VIVID VISION

VIVID
VISION

**A REMARKABLE TOOL FOR
ALIGNING YOUR BUSINESS AROUND
A SHARED VISION OF THE FUTURE**

CAMERON HEROLD

LIONCREST
PUBLISHING

VIVID VISION
A Remarkable Tool for Aligning Your Business
Around a Shared Vision of the Future

ISBN   978-1-61961-877-0   *Hardcover*
          978-1-61961-876-3   *Ebook*

This book, and all my work, is done with love and thanks for my two boys, Aidan and Connor.

CONTENTS

THE CURRENT LANDSCAPE

PICTURE THIS: You're CEO of a company. Your product is a leader in a growing market. You've got a great team. Your customers love you. You are perfectly set up to explode, and you're ready to lead this growth. You know exactly what has to happen, who needs to do what, and how to get to the next level.

There's just one problem: No one in the organization can read your mind.

Just because you know what needs to happen doesn't mean that anyone else does. Of course you can tell them, but how often do they really understand exactly what you're saying? They might understand the words, but do they really see your vision? And do they understand it well enough to execute it?

I see this all the time when coaching CEOs. They have a great team, and they are all working really, *really* hard, but at the end of the day, they aren't going anywhere.

And it's usually because the CEO has not laid out a clear map with a clear destination, so the employees don't really know where they're going. And as the saying goes, if you don't know the destination, any road will take you there.

For a business, taking any road is a road map to disaster.

The only way to have your team aligned—moving in the same direction at the same speed—is to develop a detailed vision of the future and share it with them. This seems obvious.

The problem is that *the way* leaders currently develop their visions of the future isn't working. The existing model—usually called a vision statement or mission statement, sometimes a vision board—sets leaders up for failure, right from the outset.

For example, a common method to create a mission statement is to gather a group of people in a room and have them write their favorite words on a whiteboard. Then everyone votes for their favorites from those. You take all those words that have been selected and mash them up into one sentence, and that mishmash is supposed to be a vision statement. That phrase is supposed to align the whole team.

I have no idea why people do this. Everyone in the meeting knows that it doesn't align anyone. Everyone knows the process and end result are a bit hokey. They know that it's simply one sentence, and it's usually so vague that is has no meaning.

They know they need more than that.

That sentence doesn't describe what actions the marketing or sales departments must take. It doesn't describe what the customers are saying about the organization, or what is being written and talked about in the media in regard to the company. One sentence is just too abstract (usually because creating them is a process taught by professors who have never actually built a business before).

You need so much more than what is captured in one sentence. You need something that, when you walk around your company, enables you easily to describe everybody's role and what is going on.

You need something vivid.

Try this exercise, right now: Imagine something you want but don't have. It could be your dream house. It could be a car you've loved your whole life. It could be a bike, a piece of furniture, or even a relationship. Pretend you have it now. Imagine yourself inside of it, using it, touching it. What stands out? What are you noticing? Describe what it looks like, how it feels. Describe the features, the lighting, the flow, the energy, the feel of it.

That's a pretty clear vision, isn't it?

This is what you need to do for your company.

This is the Vivid Vision.

One sentence can never do justice to this kind of all-encompassing experience. It's impossible to squeeze the level of detail necessary into a handful of words.

But with a Vivid Vision, you can. A Vivid Vision helps you steer your company in the right direction and at exactly the right speed so you can grow and attain your goals.

After decades of building companies and coaching close to one hundred others, I've finally codified this critical missing piece to growing a company.

As a leader, you likely already have this sort of deep, clear vision for where and how you want the company to grow. But it's an exercise in frustration when other people in your company can't seem to grasp what that picture is. Equally frustrating is when your people fail to become as excited and enthusiastic about it. Their lack of vision or lack of enthusiasm is because they can't see what you see.

A mission statement is just that: a statement.

But a Vivid Vision is a three-dimensional world that you can step into and explore. It's a world you can share with your team to create true alignment and amazing results. It's a true road map that helps your team see where to go, so they can figure out how to get there.

THE ORIGINS OF THE VIVID VISION

In the late 1990s, an Olympic coach explained to me

how he instructed high-performance athletes to visualize themselves performing their respective events. He encouraged them to see and feel themselves acting in that crucial moment.

Extrapolating that technique, he knew that if he could train business owners to see and feel themselves performing like an athlete, their businesses would operate at the same high-functioning level. He created that concept of leaning out into the future, and I liked it so much that I simply co-opted it to use for business.

When I came upon this invaluable tool, I was working for a private currency company. I began using the technique there, and then joined 1-800-GOT-JUNK? as the chief operating officer. There, I envisioned a big, audacious goal: to double the company's revenue in three years. Initially, I didn't know *how* we would do it, but I was confident that our team would handle the operational requirements necessary to make it an actuality.

We just had to give them the Vivid Vision (at the time, we called it a Painted Picture), the direction to which the company was headed.

We met our goal—in just under three years. In fact

we doubled our revenue every year for the six years I was COO.

Throughout my career, I've helped build three companies to over $100 million and coached dozens of entrepreneurs and CEOs to do the same (or better), and I've used the power of the Vivid Vision to completely transform each of those organizations.

Right now, you're three years away from accomplishing your own equally big and audacious goal. You may not believe me, but it's true.

If you trust the process I'm going to walk you through in this book, you'll get there.

PART ONE

WHY YOU NEED A VIVID VISION

———

A SHARED VISION

THE OLD ADAGE SAYS that a picture is worth a thousand words. And that's merely one static picture. What if I showed you a scene in a movie? By taking that picture and putting it into motion, it gives you who-knows-how-many new words to describe it.

A scene from *The Sound of Music* will demonstrate what I mean. There is an iconic, unforgettable scene in which Julie Andrews twirls and sings in an Alpine meadow surrounded by mountains. Wearing a staid, simple black-and-white dress, she appears enraptured by the beauty of nature as she belts out, "The hills are alive with the sound of music." Her playful frolicking evolves into a reverential awe, reflecting her deep spirituality.

If you've ever watched the scene, you can probably visualize it shot for shot. You might even find yourself singing along, maybe in a cheesy falsetto.

But if you've never seen it, you might imagine something vastly different from the actual scene I just described. And that was a pretty good description.

Even with the paragraph I provided, it is impossible for someone who has not seen the movie to accurately envision the scene the rest of us have in our minds.

This is how vividly you need to think about the vision for your business. It might be crystal clear to you—every shot in the scene, every word in the song—but everyone else is blind and deaf when it comes to the stuff in your head. And a sentence or a paragraph is not going to make them see the light or hear the music.

No one else in your organization knows with any certainty what it is you want to build. At best, they guess. If you want your team to build what you see, you must provide them with the means of understanding it. Otherwise, you will get different ideas of what to build. Everyone will grasp a part, but no one will put it all together. No one will comprehend what you want to build as a whole.

The result? Confusion. Everyone will have a unique, subjective experience, drawing a picture that looks nothing like anyone else's.

In other words, your workplace is without alignment. No alignment means no growth (or, at best, boring 7% growth per year, rather than the hyper-growth we all want and deserve).

LAYING OUT A VISION IS LIKE BUILDING A HOUSE

Another way of looking at this miscommunication problem is to imagine that you're a contractor who wants to build a house for me. Suppose I tell you I want a 6,000-square-foot house with a nice porch and a beautiful outside landscape. How could you build a house from that one-sentence description? It is so vague that it's nearly useless.

You might have the best construction crew on the planet, but if that's all the instructions you get from me, who knows what they will create. Part of the crew might start building a Midcentury Modern house, someone else may start on a Victorian home, another person may build a Tudor mansion, while yet another person opts for a Cape Cod style. Each aspect of the house is going to be radically different from the others. And even if everyone is aligned, it's almost certainly not going to be what I envisioned in my mind.

Now, imagine if I described my home in five detailed pages. I explain the color of the house, the kinds of trees, the wainscoting, the layout of the porch, the positioning of the windows, and so on. You can draw a picture from that level of detail that will be very close to what I have in my head.

You might be laughing at this example, but I see this sort of misalignment all the time. And if you have anything close to this in your company, it will create frustration because people working toward a common goal absolutely must be on the same page. Like rowers in a boat, if you are rowing in different directions, you will end up going around in circles. This is fuel for arguments and infighting. This is how office politics and drama get started.

Moreover, this is how time gets wasted. When management has to spend time putting out fires and adjusting alignment, the company is essentially spinning its wheels but going nowhere—or worse, moving quickly but in reverse. Nobody's three-year plan calls for constant realignment.

THE SOLUTION

EMPLOYEES NATURALLY WANT to perform well and feel good about the work they contribute. They want their company to be a success.

If, as the leader of the organization, you're not providing your team with the same insight into your vision for the company (so they can help you get the company there!), you're holding them back.

You are the problem, not them.

When people show up for work, knowing—not guessing—exactly what their chief executive envisions for the company three years out, down to the minor details, they're aligned. And aligned workers perform better than individuals merely operating in proximity toward a vague goal that might be a month or ten years out, not that it makes any difference either way.

When an employee understands that their actions over the next three years will have an impact, by making even just one of the aims written into the Vivid Vision come to fruition, that person is motivated to make that happen.

The benefits to employees of a Vivid Vision don't stop there, however. This company-wide alignment also aids your team in becoming decision-makers themselves. One goal as the company leader is to develop leaders within the organization. The more work you can responsibly delegate, the more you can focus on bigger issues. One hallmark of a good company is the ability to promote from within, which leads to a culture of trust, dedication, and willingness.

A company that can achieve a foxhole-type unity is generally headed for success. When everyone knows their particular assignment, they can function without having to try to do someone else's job, which inevitably results in failing at their own responsibilities.

Suppose you have a car filled with a couple of young drivers and their parents that's headed from New

York to Los Angeles. If the parents fall asleep, and a young man takes the wheel, while he may not know the whole route, he at least knows to drive west. He can make this decision on his own without having to wake his parents to ask, "Mom, Dad, are we OK to keep driving west?"

He also knows that he can drive slightly southwest because, well, he has seen a map of the United States. Furthermore, he knows that he could stop along the way because he understands it's a long journey and he's not expected to make it cross-country in one burst. Besides, by his taking the wheel, the family will make much better time than expected, so it's no big deal if they want to stop and enjoy the scenery.

The point of this story is, when you know where you're going, you can make decisions and apply them.

Again, the reason companies spend so much time managing people, holding them accountable and running a permission-based system, is because nobody knows where they're going. They don't even know the revenue goal or the operating budget. Everyone is doing an individual job without understanding its ultimate purpose and how that role ties into the bigger picture.

A sentence, no matter how descriptive or inspiring,

will not—it cannot—align a company. For that matter, neither can a vision board. The concept behind the vision board is a set of pictures, which, as we know, each paint a thousand words. You put those pictures on a bulletin board, and the idea is that they will add up, create synergy, and spark a clear vision.

In fact, a vision board can be very good for doing exactly that—for *you*. But if I look at your vision board, I will probably see something entirely different. The vision board is only meant for one individual person. Those pictures are each worth a thousand words, but the words you extrapolate and the words I extrapolate are inevitably bound to diverge. The more people who "read" that vision board, the more interpretations you'll get.

One of my old vision boards, which I hung above my desk, featured a picture of an antique wooden table with a pair of champagne glasses on it. If I were to show that vision board to ten people, I would get ten unique interpretations, which makes it a rather useless alignment tool.

People are bound to focus on the wrong aspects without more clarity from me. One person may look at the vision board and think the wooden table was the centerpiece, representing a celebration of a rustic way of life. Someone else may conclude that I literally wanted an old table with champagne glasses.

Everyone would miss the metaphorical significance. My vision board signified that I wanted to be with someone special and celebrate special occasions with them. Whether it involved drinking champagne or a romantic dinner somewhere secluded, it didn't matter.

Because we interpret things differently, the vision board is a horrible tool for aligning more than one person.

The written word, on the other hand, is much more precise and less easily misconstrued.

There is—or at least ought to be—clarity in written material. You'll want to continually polish the Vivid Vision until you remove all ambiguity. That may mean bringing in a writer or an editor to hone those words into a clear, articulate, and comprehensible document.

I said the statements made in the Vivid Vision should be clear and free of ambiguity, so let me be clear by differentiating this tool from a forecast. Forecasting is a method of looking at your current numbers and estimating goals based on those figures. Estimating isn't a part of the Vivid Vision.

On the one hand, the Vivid Vision is about precision, but on the other, it's based on the future, not on where you currently stand. The focus is on where you intend to be three years down the road, regardless of where you might be now.

CHAPTER 3

THE "BHAG"

SUPPOSE FOR A MOMENT that five years ago, you and I considered how to build an incredible electric car. We may have used the Prius as our base model and decided to make it drive just a little bit faster. That is, of course, a very practical and viable method of furthering technology.

But that's not the only way.

Compare that to the Tesla Model S. It's about as far from a Prius as you can get, yet it's an electric car, too. When Elon Musk considered building an electric car, he could have chosen the status quo. But instead, he projected a vision into the future of what he wanted, rather than taking the current model and forecasting it forward. A Tesla seats seven people, not because

Musk started with a Prius and decided to make it bigger, but because he wanted an insanely fast luxury car also capable of seating his five children.

I've known Elon for more than two decades. He's a great example of envisioning what is possible and then setting out to build it, rather than basing his creations on the current state of affairs.

The point of creating a Vivid Vision is to lean out into the future, to pretend you're traveling in a time machine to a moment three years ahead. It's dreaming where you want the company to be in every metric, from personnel to review to location to services, and working backward from there. Most companies do the opposite—they look at where they actually are and make designs based solely on that.

There's a BHAG (pronounced "bee-hag") quality to the Vivid Vision. BHAG is a term developed by Jim Collins. In his landmark book, *Good to Great*, he talked about having Big, Hairy, Audacious Goals (BHAG). These goals require you to stretch your imagination to such an extent that people outside of the company probably think you're crazy. But the people inside your company believe those goals are quite possible—if they share in your Vivid Vision.

The BHAG is a goal that by its very nature works to align an organization. Thirty years ago, Microsoft had a BHAG to place a computer on every desktop. Bear in mind that, at this point, they didn't even make computers! That is a pretty big, hairy, and audacious goal, right? What they realized was that the better the software they created, the more they could actually make that dream a reality.

A company's BHAG is as important as its Core Values. And its Vivid Vision, which articulates that BHAG, is just as important, if not more so.

In 1961, President John F. Kennedy announced that by the end of the decade, the United States would put a man on the moon. Think about that for a moment. That may seem like small potatoes now, but President Kennedy's announcement was an extraordinary, almost unimaginable statement, especially given that the computers of the time were so primitive that we'd hardly recognize them today.

Sometimes, the BHAG aspect of a Vivid Vision requires you to imagine tools and technology that may not even exist today, except in the imaginations of some very creative thinkers. Or you'll have to envision what society may look like in three years.

When creating the Vivid Vision, don't worry about *how* it is going to happen, only *that* it's going to happen. It's the CEO's job to figure out *where* the organization is going. It's the role of the leadership team to figure out *how* they will make the Vivid Vision happen. President Kennedy didn't sit down and map out exactly how to put a man on the moon; he just decided that was the direction the country was headed.

If you imagine big enough, you'll meet some doubters. If you told your employees that you want to design an electric car that can go 300 miles on a single charge, go from 0 to 60 miles per hour in three seconds flat, seat seven comfortably, and look as sexy as an Aston Martin, somebody will say, "There's no way."

That tells you you're on the right track.

After you set the BHAG, break it down into chunks. The chunks represent the individual steps in a process that will eventually get you from point A to the BHAG. So, in the case of building a home, you would break it down into the different steps of pouring the foundation, wiring the electrical, hooking up the plumbing, and so on. Step by step, the giant, almost indigestible task becomes manageable one component at a time.

Think about the old Chinese proverb that asks, "How

do you eat an elephant?" You do it one bite at a time.

That is the same way you tackle your Vivid Vision. Once you accomplish a statement within the plan, the path forward becomes clearer, and another statement can be worked on.

A THREE-YEAR VISION

Why three years? Why not one? Why not five? What makes three the magic number?

The reality is that if you venture too far into the future, the vision becomes very foggy. The further out you go, the more chaos is thrown into the mix, and it becomes very difficult to see your company with any degree of clarity. Who knows what the world will look like in ten years? Did anyone really expect the drastic changes that occurred between 2006 and 2016? Or, for that matter, between 1996 and 2006?

On the other hand, if you only stick your toes in the water and look only one or two years into the future, nothing earth-shattering has time to transpire.

Moreover, that small a goal does nothing to inspire. If your Vivid Vision is going to set the world on fire, at least as far as your business goes, then it has to rock the boat a little. You need to wow people inside and outside your company.

Additionally, the three-year goal inspires innovation. Not only is time stretched, but imagination is stretched, as well. When people sit down and actually have to figure out how they're going to get from here to there, they're reassured that they have a stretch of time to take chances, even if the chances do not pan out. That luxury of failure—and it is a luxury while also being a necessity—allows the engineers of your Vivid Vision to think outside the box, and to try novel methods or tactics that would be impossible under pending deadlines.

This amount of time additionally allows for you to attack projects on your own schedule, rather than having that timeline dictated to you by necessity.

To illustrate that idea, go back to the home we're building. Some projects must be in place in a particular order, but while you're working on those foundational pieces, you can have other work done, too. For instance, while you wait to have the custom doors carved and installed, you may decide to get special handmade doorknobs added, instead of buying off-the-shelf models. Three years is the perfect balance between realistic and achievable, and it gives you the chance to work on different aspects simultaneously.

SAMPLE VIVID VISION: COO ALLIANCE CITY FORUMS (2020)

The following is our 2020 Vivid Vision for the COO Alliance City Forums. Creating a Vivid Vision brings the future into the present, so we can have clarity on what we are building now. It is a detailed overview of what the COO Alliance City Forums will look like, feel like, and act like—by December 31, 2020. Sharing it with others helps it become reality!

CORE VALUES

· People Come First
· Be Open-Minded
· Innovation Is Key
· Come Ready to Collaborate

CULTURE

Culture is our top priority. We create an environment and membership that exemplifies our core values as leaders in our own companies.

We take our interview process very seriously and vet most importantly for culture fit. Members must also meet requirements regarding their company size and position in the company.

We deliver a first-class peer group for our members by spending time interviewing each and every member to ensure they are brilliant (but humble), eager to collaborate and see others succeed, agile in the way they lead their business, and innovative in their thought process.

We strive for diversity. We know that coos come from different backgrounds, and that their combined experiences strengthen the coo Alliance. As long as our members share our values, the more diverse the background, the better, as this enriches their peers' experience and opportunities to innovate and grow.

EMPLOYEES

A killer culture starts at the top. We take vetting our chairs as seriously as vetting our members. The city chairs set the tone for the meetings and their group. While they do not mentor or coach, they play the role of facilitator and ensure that events stay engaging and relevant. Quality chairs ensure that our values are upheld at the City Forum level.

Our employees are entirely remote and manage all aspects of the company including chair relations, annual visits for branding, and social compliance, as well as social media, tech, billing and onboarding, and interviewing support.

MEMBERS

This is the only network of its kind in the WORLD for those who are second-in-command. Members love that we are not simply an exclusive social club where the main qualification is who you know and how much you make. We care about helping them find people who not only understand the issues their company is facing, but who also want to collaborate. They find our philosophy and values refreshing and are eager to add value and support to our community.

The ideal member is someone who is already successful but needs support and is ready to learn how to grow their people as well as their company.

Members love that they have finally found their tribe. We're not just another peer group for entrepreneurs or key executives who aren't truly the backup for the CEO, but rather we're a place exclusively dedicated to seconds-in-command.

Members are applying faster than we used to be able to interview them, so we've automated and outsourced parts of our process to scale rapidly, while maintaining our entrepreneurial environment.

PEER-TO-PEER MASTERMIND PERFECTION

We know from experience that the true value to membership is getting to know our peers, and tapping into their experiences and knowledge from having faced, and conquered, the same issues every other member is facing.

Members not only get to know their peers at the events through collaborative breakouts, group problem solving, and peer presentations, but they also get to tour hosting members' offices, understand their processes, and see their culture in action.

Members also have access to two accountability partners whom they connect with regularly to share ideas and help hold each other accountable.

WORLD-CLASS CONTENT

The content from the coo Alliance events comes in a variety of forms. Content areas we cover include the following:

- The CEO–COO relationship
- Operations and execution
- People: recruiting, interviewing, topgrading, onboarding, handcuffs, and offboarding
- Culture: All areas of turning companies into mag-

nets for great employees
- Technology tools to accelerate growth
- Leadership and skill development
- Meetings
- Strategic thinking and planning
- Coaching and delegation
- And more...

CITY FORUM EVENTS

- 6 events per year, per City Forum group
- 10–14 members per City Forum group (not including the City Forum chair)
- Cities and regions can have more than one City Forum—pending regional needs.
- Cities and regions can have more than one City Forum chair also.

We now have chairs representing City Forums in each of the top 30 populated US cities.

The COO Alliance City Forums are a huge support to the COOs of small and midsized companies. Many COOs attending the City Forums begin attending our National Program held in Scottsdale.

We provide the innovative seconds-in-command with the resources and support they require for healthy and rapid expansion of their companies. In doing so, we help create millions of jobs where employees are treated with respect and valued for their work.

The 6 City Forum events annually are truly unique and provide members with a chance to

- Take a step back from the daily grind and think strategically, see their business with fresh eyes, and make the changes necessary to achieve rapid expansion and success
- Discover peer perfection where we provide members with a room of subject-matter experts in many fields who will help them in every area of their business that they are looking to develop
- Receive immediate support and solutions to issues they are facing, allowing them to leave every event with answers, resources, and an actionable step-by-step plan

We operate the meetings in a confidential environment that allows everyone to feel comfortable in truly sharing and opening up with each other. Members run presentations to the group on areas where they feel stuck and receive feedback from each other. We work through a variety of forms, worksheets, and exercises to encourage members to be introspective and grow themselves and their companies.

ONLINE REGIONAL CHAIR MEETINGS

Quarterly regional chair meetings are held online to discuss their state of affairs with their peers and the National Program. These calls provide a platform for them to get support from the National Program, share ideas with one another, identify issues and trends, and innovate to improve their City Forum members' experiences.

MEDIA

The media is buzzing about us. They constantly talk about our online programs, the City Forums, and the National Program. They highlight our innovative priorities, program structure, and vetting process. We're recognized for not being solely interested in large-sized companies, but focused on helping coos grow on every level.

When companies want to grow, their second-in-command joins the coo Alliance. The media also turns to us and our members as subject-matter experts for articles on all areas of business growth. We are constantly getting interviewed about how we have managed to attract such an amazing group of coos, chairs, and team members.

We are seen as one of the top mastermind groups

in the world for growing companies. We have people in the program who are constantly being recognized for turning their companies into gold mines with amazing cultures overnight.

Our program is seen as equal to or better than an MBA on a resume with what people are able to accomplish after joining. In fact, the media has often referred to the COO Alliance as a real-world MBA for seconds-in-command.

We are viewed as the only leadership growth option for COOs and are known for breeding leaders who are innovative, forward-thinking, strategic, and possess a human-centric work focus with rapid company growth and expansion.

SYSTEMS

We have an online portal and Slack channel for individual City Forum groups to

- View meeting notes
- Post questions
- Share relevant content

We also have a Slack channel and portal for chairs to share resources. All portal and channel activities are monitored by the chair to assure quality and organization.

BRAND

When the COO Alliance is talked about, the City Forums, online programs, and National Programs are all talked about together. There is, however, a strong distinction within our membership between being in the City Forum and also being invited for National Membership. The COO Alliance is a forward-thinking brand that builds strong COOs by providing them with the resources, tools, and ongoing support to develop and grow their people, businesses, and bottom lines.

PART TWO

HOW TO WRITE IT

———

PREPARING TO WRITE

TO BEGIN THE PROCESS of creating your Vivid Vision, your first job is to free your mind from the day-to-day worries of running your business.

That means leaving the office. Grab a notepad and a pen, and go somewhere inspiring. Outside, for a number of reasons, is an ideal place to allow yourself to dream, to hop into your time machine and lean out into the future.

And no, it won't work if you shut your office door or go to a conference room to work. You will get distracted if you stay in the building. And you will likely get dragged into mundane tasks.

But when you head to a lake house or a mountain cabin, you're away from horns and honks of rushing traffic outside the office building and the equally distracting pedestrian traffic inside. You want to leave the trite motivational posters, the ticking clock, the endless cubicles, and the fluorescent lights behind you. Getting away from your office means no telephones ringing, no office machinery humming, no repair technicians banging, no custodians sweeping, and no employees asking you questions. Even if you sit in your backyard enjoying the warmth of the sun, it's better than writing your Vivid Vision on a plane or from your office.

Make it just you and a notepad, and maybe a meadow or a pond.

Outdoors, you can access a different mindset. The natural world completely expands your spectrum of thought. You feel connected to the whole universe. You feel the fresh air and the grass under your feet, and you just...relax. I think we've all experienced that feeling.

A vacation is a really great time to write a Vivid Vision. On vacation, your mind is completely relaxed and open. When you enter this state, your mind can wander.

Another thing you gain by leaving the office and entering nature is freedom from the internet.

Notice that I said to grab a pad of paper and pen to write your Vivid Vision. I didn't say to type it on the computer. There's a good reason for this. Trying to disconnect with a computer in front of you is an exercise in futility. Temptation will have you checking your email or Twitter feed to find out what's going on. You'll wonder about something and will want to Google it immediately.

Before long, you're going down a rabbit hole, having been sucked back into the daily grind. A business environment triggers a response in the brain that over time becomes routine: *"How are we going to do this?"* *"What if that?"* *"How does this bring about that?"* and on and on ad nauseum.

The Vivid Vision, on the other hand, is a fantastical journey into an uncharted realm, requiring you to unlock the playful part of your mind that is so easily hijacked in an office.

Remember that this is neither the time nor the place to think about how you're going to do this. Again, to go back to the home-building metaphor, think of yourself as the homeowner who is envisioning the perfect house. It's not your job to pick up a hammer and nails; you have trained professionals to do that. Your job is to communicate to the professionals what you want—they will construct it, wire it, paint it, and do everything else that is necessary to make your dream home real.

Business thinking is pragmatic thinking, and pragmatic thinking is not what we are aiming for when we lean out into the future. It's difficult to imagine anything unique or novel, or for that matter anything out of the ordinary, in the enclosed, well-trod office environment.

Not only that, but there is also a tendency to compromise by thinking pragmatically. We end up wondering, *"What does the market want?" "What would the buyers be looking for?" "What do the venture capitalists want to fund?"*

That other-centric thinking is great most of the time—but not now. This is a chance to engage in some childlike dreaming.

This really is a personal experience. As the head of a company, it's your duty to provide vision, which you must then communicate to your team. And then you must build that team accordingly, hiring like-minded people and letting go of anyone who acts as an obstacle to the completion of your vision. And then, once you have your best team in place, who see the same vision of the future you want to create, this personal endeavor becomes a shared adventure.

Athletes use visualization not only in the moments prior to their events, whether that be on a golf course or on a football field, but at all hours of the day and in a variety of locations. They might lie in bed and picture the ideal jump shot over and over again, or they might visualize themselves skiing the perfect run, aware of every part of their body, smelling the alpine air, hearing the roar of the crowd.

Wherever their zone of tranquility is, athletes who incorporate visualization techniques will go to that place to rehearse their performance, so that on game day, they merely duplicate what they have already witnessed themselves doing time and time again.

I use this technique when I go on stage. If I'm attending a speaking event, I will walk out onto the stage or into the auditorium the day before, and I will visualize the crowds of people gathered in front of me. I will see myself standing on that stage, ready to speak. I will get the feel of the space. I will allow myself to be comfortable in the room.

The following day, when I have to return and actually perform, I feel as if I have done it before. Then, it's just a matter of repeating that same activity.

Start your Vivid Vision this way: calm, relaxed, and envisioning a world you'd love to help create and be part of some day.

CHAPTER 5

A DIFFERENT KIND OF EXERCISE

ENTREPRENEURS SPEND too much time worrying about how something is going to happen. As a result, they lose their ability to dream about something great. In fact, what they lose is the creative process.

When Elon Musk was dreaming about his Tesla Model S, he didn't care how it happened; those thoughts would have impeded something that did not yet exist.

He only cared that it be a fast, ultra-stylish vehicle that ran on clean energy and fit the size of his family. As long as those criteria were met, he didn't care how the car was built. Had he worried about the practicalities and listened to the consensus opinions of the time in the beginning, he certainly would have lost his inspiration.

Just like Elon, you want to figure out what the goal is first and then work backward—with a talented team of brilliant pros—to figure out how you're going to make that happen.

One technique I recommend you use is the Mind Map. This is a visual way to organize information. The idea is to start in the center and work out from there with little branches. So, to visualize something a little more tangible, think about a tree trunk growing in the Earth's inner core with its branches stretching out and into the sky; each of those branches contain twigs, which extend farther out. The Mind Map works in a similar way: a core that branches out into smaller components.

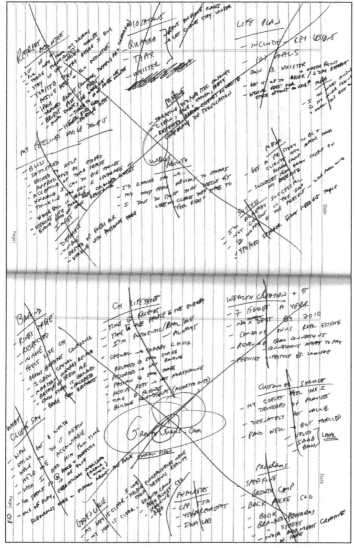

The Mind Map I did for my first Vivid Vision when I started BackPocket COO (which I was originally going to call Growth Guru).

Now, apply this to the world of business. As the leader of an organization, you are firmly planted in the center, and the various areas that contribute to the business branch out—marketing, sales, engineering, and so forth. With that image in place, build off of that by describing those branches in about three or four bullet points each. In other words, describe what your marketing looks like, and sales, and so on, until you've captured every area.

Remember, too, that among the branches of your business, you want to consider every aspect of the organization—the culture, the vibe, the informal codes of conduct, the fiscal environment, the scenery—all of that. Deliberately leave out numbers and data. Get a feel for the place. When you step out of your time machine three years from now and walk around the office, what's happening? What can you say that is typical of the business three years from now?

The Mind Map is the initial foray into the Vivid Vision and will act as an outline for the rough draft that you the leader will then write. Look three years out and describe each of the branches of your business as you ideally see them. Remember, the idea is to get the thoughts out, no matter how seemingly crazy. You can worry about fleshing them out later.

Describe your marketing department, IT, finance, sales, and operations. Describe your culture, what your employees are saying about you, and what the media is writing about you. Describe the details of every area in your business until you've exhausted all the goals that are hiding in the back of your mind.

It's like the dream home: Your job is to dream about what the home can look like; the architect and the engineer will figure out how to make that happen.

Also, keep in mind that this vision has to be grand enough to inspire your team. All too often companies ask, "How big can we grow?" instead of, "How big do we want to get?" which would naturally lead to the next question, "How do we get there?" Rather than aiming to double the company's growth in three years, they simply look at projections and forecast a 7% or 8% growth rate and use that figure as a benchmark.

The Vivid Vision, as I stated earlier, is a personal experience. It requires a visionary to conceive it and deliver it. The CEO must be the one to put the vision into words. Although others can weigh in and provide insights, you cannot delegate this responsibility to someone else in the company.

You also don't want this process to be a kumbaya

campfire group hug—if you get everybody together and merge all of their ideas, the Vivid Vision will be too watered down. It's like getting seven people to decide where to go for dinner, with the goal of making everyone happy. In the end, you either settle on something bland or you cancel plans to go out.

The Vivid Vision is, in a way, a fragile instrument. Like a piece of delicate art, it requires delicate handling. You must carefully articulate it in such a way that it informs and inspires. By nature, most entrepreneurs aren't writers. Therefore, it's important to have that initial visionary statement honed by someone with deft writing skills. Generally, it's best to hire a professional.

To be clear, though, the rough draft has to be there. The vision must be fleshed out and put down on paper before you bring in a writer. Once you have something to work with, then it can be polished to a sparkling shine. I'm not a writer by trade, but I have people for that, just as you have people who fix the computers, make cold calls, vacuum the floors, or whatever else the business requires.

Once the document is worded precisely to your satisfaction, then spice it up with some stylish graphic design. Think of this as your company Bible, so take pride in it. You want to use graphic design elements from your website or your marketing materials (if you can), or anything that will inspire the reader without distracting them. Consider including your logo, your color palette, or anything else that identifies the Vivid Vision with your company's brand.

Try to keep the finished product to four pages of content or less. You're going to send this out to potential and current employees, suppliers, and customers. Everyone is going to see this document, so you want to give people something more exciting than just a plain Word document.

Three years from now, when your vision becomes reality, you'll look back on this piece of work fondly. Maybe you'll frame it or store it in a special spot to showcase it with the attention it deserves.

It is your vision, after all.

CHAPTER 6

MY FIRST VIVID VISION

I'VE WRITTEN three Vivid Vision documents over the last nine years, and I'm preparing to write my fourth.

When I began my first Vivid Vision experience, I knew I needed to go outside the box. There was no way I could create the document from inside an office or by sitting at a desk. I needed to allow my mind to wander, so I grabbed a blank notebook and a pen and headed for a hammock in my backyard. I slid my headphones on and let the sounds of the Grateful Dead lull me into relaxation. In fact, I'm listening to them now as I proofread this final manuscript!

Getting away from the distractions and spending time outdoors worked so well for me. That's why I recommended it to you in the last chapter.

When I wrote my first Vivid Vision for my company, I spent about four hours exploring the Mind Map of my business. I just let my mind wander. I imagined what my business looked like three years into the future. And when an idea came to me, I wrote it down in the notebook. I described what I felt. I thought about the different components of my business, my coaching models, my brand, who my customers were, and what the media was saying about me—three years into the future. I thought about events I might run.

I allowed myself to pretend *everything* was already happening.

For example, I would close my eyes and try to visualize a speaking event. I would imagine the audience and what people might look like. I pictured the size of the rooms we were in, and the groups that hired me. I'd see all of this, and then, I'd sit up to write every detail down in the notebook as quickly as possible. Usually, I wrote down two to three ideas before closing my eyes again and daydreaming.

That first day, I spent about four hours allowing myself to listen to music while daydreaming. My only focus was on capturing the vision of my company. I never worried about how I was going to make it happen.

After four hours, I ended up with about two to three pages of rough notes, organized into random areas. When I was finished, I put the notes aside. Two days later, I picked them up once again along with my headphones, iPhone, and the pen I used a couple of days before. Armed with my tools, I returned to the hammock and spent another hour filling in the blanks, rethinking with a fresh head about each area, and adding more description to each section.

On this second pass, I considered what my core values might be like even though I was a company of one. I was trying to dream about what I wanted to build and what impact I would have on my customers. Again, I wrote it all down.

Next, I typed up my notes from those two sessions, organizing all my ideas into smaller categories. I wrote them up as bullet points. For example, under customer service I had three or four bullet points, while under the public speaking section I had five or six.

Then I took all the bullet points and wrote a paragraph for each section. This took me about an hour to draft. Then, I sent it off to a journalist, who was a really great writer and someone I had worked with in the past. He took my work and made it jump off the page, and that was it. In fact, I have a few writers I work with consistently to polish up hundreds of Vivid Visions for companies per year. If you need someone to help make your pop off the page, email me at VividVision@CameronHerold.com.

Then, I decided I wanted the document to be more visceral, more engaging. I went to a website called Upwork, where you can get graphic design work done. I hired someone to draw cartoon sketches for a bunch of different areas of my Vivid Vision. I thought the cartoons would be humorous and would add color to it, helping people to connect with it more. Now on my third Vivid Vision in nine years, I recognize that design elements and photos are better than cartoons.

My first Vivid Vision was four pages (you can see it at the end of this chapter), and I shared it with everybody. I shared it with customers, suppliers, and the media. And I kept on sharing it. I put it on my website, and I handed it out at every speaking event, giving everyone in the audience a copy.

What I started seeing was that the more people I shared my Vivid Vision with, the more that my Vivid Vision came true. I wasn't entirely aware of how much of it was coming true until I was on a call with a client and he said, "I see you just bought your chalet in Whistler. Congratulations, your Vivid Vision is coming true."

I was like, "Oh my gosh, you're right. I forgot that I had put that one in." My Vivid Vision was coming to completion. We took possession of the chalet on December 15, 2010. The three-year period in which I had envisioned the chalet would end on December 31. It had snuck in at the very end of the three-year period.

Among the other realizations of that first Vivid Vision: I began speaking at a lot of Young Presidents' Organization chapters and industry events, and I was introduced to speakers' bureaus, which started representing me. Those ideas that I had on that hammock in my yard had come to fruition, despite my having no idea how they would come to be when I put pen to paper.

In fact, I realized that it was rather easy in retrospect and that I had accomplished a lot of what I had set out to do. But at the time I wrote it down, it was a big stretch for me. But it worked because I began by setting foundations that I knew I would build on. And when I stayed focused on the vision, I started to figure out how to make it all happen.

One reason a lot of people get stuck on their career

path is because they don't think about where they want to be. They chase down ideas, but that often does not lead toward anything. Whereas someone who is thinking three years out or even ten years out—but who is taking targeted steps in the right directions—is going to take advantage of opportunities directly aligned with their goals rather than taking meandering paths, going in circles or going nowhere.

My first Vivid Vision had been a success.

SAMPLE VIVID VISION: MY FIRST VIVID VISION (2010)

The best way to ensure that dreams become reality is to take the vision from our mind and share it with people. My following vision, what I call my Vivid Vision, is a mental image of what BackPocket COO will look like, feel like, and act like by December 31, 2010.

OVERALL

"Why" I do what I do is so clear. I love helping entrepreneurs make their dreams happen. Since "Why" I do what I do is clear, "How" I do what I do is also clear. I run Growth Camps, Speaking Events, and BackPocket COO programs and sell books and DVDs that help entrepreneurs make their dreams happen. Listening to my inner voice filters my decisions for me. I call on and trust my gut. Feeling jazzed about working with an entrepreneur to make their dreams happen has my dreams unfolding, making it fun, with time and money being abundant for me. My company BackPocket COO grows because entrepreneurs keep telling each other about me and how I've helped them. Companies feel compelled to hire me to help them because "Why" I'm doing what I do resonates with them. I have an "I'd Rather Do..." list, which helps me say no to contracts I don't want because I have tons of things I'd rather do in life than work with a company that doesn't fit. I only work with clients that "fit" with me like my clothes and car do. I know when a client feels like a fit for me.

SUCCESS

I'm already successful. I feel successful every day. I no longer try to prove anything to anyone. Internally, I'm excited at how successful I already am. I don't get caught in "The GAP," because I no longer focus on the horizon to feel like I've made it. I am already there. Everything else I do and start to acquire or achieve is simply a bonus. I'm so happy in the present just being able to spend time taking the kids to school, having time midday to spend with my wife, and having frequent two- to three-hour lunches with friends mid-week. My dad's father was right.

HOW I FEEL

People keep telling me that I look so relaxed. I feel really lucky to be doing what I'm doing. My days are fun-filled and relaxing, and my time is my own. I'm excited to help entrepreneurs in every interaction I have with them. I feel appreciated by others that I work with. I comfortably accept the praise people give me, and I let it sink in. I know I make a serious difference to the success of each of my clients. I feel confident in working with companies ready to go public so I can share in their upside. I always have and continue to view life through a pair of rose-colored glasses. I'm exactly where I'm supposed to be.

MENTOR BOARD OF ADVISORS

"Thirty companies or people have already figured it out." I simply connect to those who have already figured it out and do what they did. I'm known as a "connector" because of how many people I know and regularly call on, leveraging social networks like LinkedIn and Facebook. It feels awesome being connected to and learning from such a great group called my MBA.

CULTURE AND SPIRIT

My work with entrepreneurs is a balance of play, extrasensory overload, rigorous work, and excitement around the plans and systems we build together. I only work with companies that I want my family name attached to. I have admired Milton Wong for this since I met him—I don't compromise.

BRAND/IMAGE

My brand rings true with people. When they meet me

and see my brand, they "get it." I am respected, well-liked, and people are heard saying, "I need a Cameron." My look has a Brooks Brothers confidence, J.Crew casual feel to it. People who know me constantly say, "Wow, this is such a great fit for you."

LEADERSHIP

Clients say I've helped hold them accountable to do the things they needed to do to really grow their company. Companies value me as a senior leader they can have on their team but can't afford full-time. I get results. Clients consistently say that my leadership has saved or made them millions of dollars.

COMMUNICATION

I don't have a filter—and I'm admired for that. People know they can trust me because I say exactly what's on my mind. I think out loud—and that is something I'm respected and hired for. People comment that my brand is a breath of fresh air because I say what I mean. I don't sugarcoat things. I say what people are thinking but don't feel comfortable saying. I have set up my company so office politics don't exist and everyone I work with is energetically communicating for the good of the entrepreneurs we're helping.

CUSTOMER SERVICE

My clients are very clear about my promises and feel like I deliver on them. My client companies feel lucky to have me helping them. They feel like they have paid well for my services but received great value in return. They feel like they get great value from every interaction with me. They liken hiring me to buying a safety net provided by a Volvo, the sleek designed systems to a Saab, and the mindset with which I work with them to the agility of a BMW. My clients repeatedly say they wish they had me full-time but are thrilled they have me for the time they do.

PROGRAMS

I run focused programs, which I don't deviate from. My speaking events are about Cameron Herold's leadership and growth expertise and the systems and content provided by BackPocket COO. My presentations are very Seth Godin-ish, having almost no words on the slides, allowing me to work from a "conscious stream of thought." I am a frequent speaker to YPO chapters in the USA, Canada, and internationally. My Growth Camp program happens ten times per year. The locations I host them at in Whistler, Vancouver, and Quadra Island are all top-notch. All programs are a cross between TSB, Millionaire's Club, and The Idea Factory. I've started doing one-day Growth

Camps with groups of entrepreneurs in cities I am speaking in to leverage my travel. My BackPocket COO program has received rave reviews from clients and has me working with companies that end up going public while I'm working with them. All programs have branded and trademarked modules. My books focus on leadership lessons for entrepreneurs and their teams. The books have also helped raise awareness of my personal brand.

SYSTEMS

I outsource more and more using Virtual Assistants by sending work to places like India where I can get top work done to help me and my clients at a fraction of the cost. I have learned from Jack Daly how to build my company with no full-time employees on payroll, yet having people who work full-time on commission.

MEDIA

The media regularly turns to me as an expert. The media covers what I do and shows companies my programs as a perfect example of outsourcing. After Growth Camps, I am able to generate media in clients' cities about what we did together as an added bonus for the client and further building my brand. The speaking events I do garner me local media coverage. The media coverage is shown on my website, and the list and credibility of the outlets covering me continue to add clients and build my personal brand.

PROFITABILITY

I make a lot of money doing what I do. I have my programs structured to be paid in advance. I have long-term programs in place with equity and stock options with clients allowing me to participate in the upside I help create. We have no family debt. I earn over seven figures a year net, and I semi-retired at forty-five years old. I am on track to have enough passive income streams and savings so that by the time I am fifty I can begin working more with socially entrepreneurial ventures. BackPocket COO owns resort properties that my family will use for generations, helping us build a strong family like Thunder Beach did. My network pays me residuals for work that I'm able to generate for them.

MY FAMILY AND FRIENDS

I regularly spend time with friends and family before I'd think of working. I only go on the road to be in cities I want to go to or to cities I can take family or friends with me. We take what others think of as long chunks of holiday time together each year. I work on building relationships with my friends old and new, and I proactively pick up the phone to call them just to say hi. Fitness is back as a part of my life, and I spend time weekly running, golfing, playing tennis, or skiing. I go hiking every summer. I spend time with people who are positive, and I regularly "fire" the negative people from my life if they haven't learned "The Secret." I include my family and friends in my 101 Goals and try to be a part of theirs also.

PART THREE

HOW TO ROLL IT OUT

———

CHAPTER 7

INTERNAL ROLLOUT

YOU'RE GOING TO roll this vision of yours out for the world to see, so be bold when you do.

When others read your Vivid Vision, they need to experience a moment of awe and wonder. If their jaws don't drop a little bit, you need to think bigger. Small, safe, calculated plans don't inspire.

Imagine the room when Elon Musk announced that he wanted his Tesla Model S to go from 0 to 60 in 2.8 seconds on something called "ludicrous mode." People thought, "Dude, you're crazy."

Get outside of your comfort zone. Get a little bit nervous. If you don't have butterflies, no one else will.

And you really want others to share in your enthusiasm. Ultimately, that's why you're crafting this document in the first place, not just secretly feeling warm and fuzzy from your vision board that no one else understands.

During the rollout, it's important to inform people that some points in the document will happen sooner than others. It will take three years to realize other points. And those other points may require things like technologies that will be invented, upgraded, or made affordable along the way and that in this moment don't exist. It's a stackable vision in that sense, building from foundation to floor to walls, and upward, just like the dream home.

If you forget to remind people that getting three years into the future necessitates first getting one year and then two years into it, they will likely overlook that obviousness and assume you're just nuts. It's a little bit like telling a thirteen-year-old what it's going to be like when they turn sixteen. They can't visualize what being a sixteen-year-old will feel or look like, since it's too far away from their current world, and the changes they will undergo are too enormous to understand.

SHARE WITH EVERYONE IN THE COMPANY

You'll begin with an internal rollout. This involves sharing your Vivid Vision with all of your employees, all of your board members, and anyone inside the walls of the company. You want to start with this group to ensure that everyone on the team really understands and is excited about the Vivid Vision. You want them to touch it, to feel it, to breathe it, before you take it to a bigger audience on the outside.

The people inside your company are the touch points with the outside world. Imagine what would happen if you gave a supplier the Vivid Vision first. They got excited and called an employee they regularly interact with. What would happen if your employee had no idea what your supplier was talking about? It would create an awkward and difficult situation for everyone.

I recommend waiting at least a quarter before an external rollout.

When you initiate an internal rollout, you want this done in person, alongside your team. Try to get everyone in the same room. This will, of course, depend on the size of your organization. If yours is a 30-person company, you can do it with everyone at once. If yours is a 500-person company, you may want to break it by business area, meeting with each one separately. If yours is a 20,000-person organization, then you will be meeting with people in shifts.

Begin by handing everyone a hard copy of the Vivid Vision. The entire group is going to read it aloud, one at a time. One person may read a couple of sentences, then the next person a couple more, and on and on until the document is finished.

While the reading is being done, the CEO's job is to look around the room to gauge people's reactions. Notice which people appear the most engaged, excited, and invested. Notice who isn't. It's the latter group of people you have to be aware and nervous of. Red flags should go up. You may have to get them out of the organization at some point. Because all it takes is one bad apple to ruin the whole bunch. One malcontent employee can start a mutiny, rallying others against the company. If this happens, everything suddenly starts going sideways.

After the group has read through the pages, you want each employee to circle any of the sentences or phrases that most excite and inspire them. Ask them to share their thoughts with the group.

This is not a forum for discussion or debate. This activity exists for employees to simply understand where the CEO wants to lead the organization. In later meetings, there will be opportunities to discuss how each statement will be accomplished, but for now, this material just needs to sink in and provide a source of contemplation and inspiration. By getting your people to think, *"What if?"* they become engaged and aligned.

Bear in mind—and I know I keep repeating this—that your journey is three years long. Each new quarter, you will want to break out the Vivid Vision again and reread it. Open it as a Word document, and highlight in green any of the sentences that have come true since the last quarter. Then, highlight in yellow any of the sentences you're currently working on.

Now, everyone will begin to see the future taking shape!

Next, take a look at each sentence and decide what projects need to be tackled next chronologically and what actions are necessary to bring them to fruition. This will help determine what your quarter is going to look like, and you can chart that course accordingly with these sentences acting as a map.

This exercise will keep everyone in the organization on the same page and in alignment. It will inspire them once again and help to keep their focus. It allows everyone to start figuring out what needs to be done today, to fulfill the lofty goals you've set in the Vivid Vision.

If you have been bold enough in your ideas, this will have two effects: It will attract and repel others. Notice I said it will attract *and* repel, not *or*. Your Vivid Vision should behave like a magnet, drawing some people in and pushing others—hopefully not too many—away. If your scope is too small, too milquetoast, or too watered down, or if everyone *likes* it, no one will love it. If this is the case, you have failed.

BE REVOLUTIONARY, NOT EVOLUTIONARY

Remember when Apple launched the iPhone seven years ago? People thought the company had gone crazy because the iPhone lacked a keyboard. "How can you release a smartphone that doesn't have a keyboard? That is absurd," people said.

However, lots of people loved it. Not only did they love it; they loved it *a lot*, branding themselves as loyal and devoted Apple customers, standing in long lines for product launches and developing a community of like-minded consumers.

Meanwhile, those who hated the keyboard-free iPhone saw the effect the device had on the rest of the industry. This prompted other companies to copy the design and compete in a market that Apple had conquered. They began to realize that keyboards would soon be as obsolete as VCRs, and eventually they were forced to convert, either willingly or kicking and screaming.

Had Apple tried to make everybody happy when it designed the revolutionary phone, they would have simply made a more polished version of the existing Blackberry. Apple's boldness in vision is what you should strive for if you want to inspire people. And remember: There will be backlash. After all, the future is scary to people who have become too comfortable in the present.

THE FIFTEEN PERCENT

I worked for a client years ago in Vancouver. As we did the internal rollout for his company, the CEO stood up and said, "About 15% of you will hate what you hear. You're not going to like what the future has in store for you, but that's OK. It's probably the right time for you to quit."

Sure enough, about 15% of his company did, in fact,

quit. Two years later, it ranked as the number-two company to work for in British Columbia (incidentally, the number-one company to work for was another client of mine who had also inspired everyone with a bold Vivid Vision).

It's OK to lose people because of the Vivid Vision. Those aren't the people you want around in the first place. It's better to know this on day one, than to spend two years trying to align and inspire them.

The same is true of potential employees. Your potential employees are going to read your document and either think, *"Hell yeah, I want to interview here,"* or, *"Hell no, I don't want to go anywhere near that place."* Now, you're not wasting time interviewing those people who aren't a good fit, much less spending money because you hired them. At the end of the day, when everyone can see where you're going, you will save time and money.

One last point on this matter: The Vivid Vision is like the Ten Commandments in that it is set in stone. The only time it should ever change is if there is literally a massive and unexpected industry transformation or if your company is going through a 90-degree pivot. Or if a global financial crisis strikes and your world gets turned upside down. Or if your building collapses.

Otherwise, remember that you are like a ship crossing the ocean, tacking left and right and dodging icebergs when necessary, but always you move in the same general direction.

Don't worry if a few sentences become moot along the way. Just let them be. This document is a beacon of light, safely guiding your crew.

EXTERNAL ROLLOUT

NOW THAT EVERYONE within the organization fully understands and is rallying behind the Vivid Vision, it's time to share it with the rest of the world. The external rollout helps everyone understand the organization's direction. It tells them why that's exciting, and why they should base their perspective of the company on that point, three years from now, rather than today.

Just as with the internal rollout among your team, it's critical to ease the minds of people who may think the idea sounds crazy. Reassure them that some concepts are still a year or two away, and that once those things are in place, the final components will not seem so far-fetched.

Introduce the Vivid Vision to them by saying, "This is what our company is going to look like in the near future. We all recognize it doesn't look like this today, but this is us leaning out three years ahead, describing what it looks, acts, and feels like."

You'll want the rollout of your Vivid Vision to happen simultaneously with everyone. This is done with email blasts, a post on the company website, newsletters, press conferences, journalist pitches, flyers, bullhorns, stopping people on the street—OK, there might be a limit to how far you go to get the message out, but definitely err on the side of too much information, rather than not enough.

The key is to continually send it to people so that everybody can see what you're building, where you're going, and what it looks like. What ends up happening is these outside parties play a role in your vision, as they contribute and conspire to make it come true.

There is no point in making plans for the future if you don't know what the future looks like. And because you want others to include you in their future plans, it's imperative that you always try to remind people of what that future looks like. It's just like orienting yourself in the wilderness—it's crucial to keep looking at the map to check your current location and to look at the way you intend to go.

The same is true of the Vivid Vision: It's a map of the future.

RECIPIENTS

As I said before, I think it's safe to wait one quarter before introducing the Vivid Vision to the outside world in an external rollout. Before you do this, make sure all your employees understand and embrace it. During the external rollout, you'll provide the document to customers, potential employees, suppliers, potential suppliers, bankers, lawyers, and, of course, the media.

Potential employees will read your Vivid Vision. This should either make them very excited to interview for a job, or they'll know right away that this isn't the right company for them.

With suppliers, the Vivid Vision will give them a better idea of where you're taking the company. This excites them, and often, you'll find suppliers wanting to be a part of what you're building. With the Vivid Vision, you've inspired them. Most suppliers rarely get a full picture of an organization they work with, so when you give them this level of insight into yours, then cool stuff starts to happen. They may even give you better prices because they can see where the company is going.

I've had potential customers sign contracts with me because they're so excited by what the company's future looks like. They're betting on the future of the company rather than betting on the current state of the company.

And when you take the Vivid Vision to the media, you have greater leverage. They should be writing about the future of your company, rather than its current position. When the media starts talking about what the company looks like three years out, people get excited.

Everyone wants to peek into the future, and for good reason. Whatever interaction you're going to have with a company generally involves a relationship of some kind that will last for some period of time. Even if it's something as simple as a manufacturer's warranty, you want to know that in a year's time, that company will still be standing.

Let's say you were going to rent a condo and you walked in and found the floors dirty, the walls in need of paint, and crummy lighting. You wouldn't want to rent the place, but if the owner said, "By the way, I'm putting in new floors tomorrow, I'm giving it a new paint job next week, and I'm putting in new hardware everywhere. Let me show you the place next door that was just refurbished last week."

When you walk into that condo, you think, *"Holy cow. I'm done. I'll take the place."*

What changed? You glimpsed the future. And that's the purpose of sharing the Vivid Vision with the outside world. Now others will see the same image that you can see, and it inspires and excites them, too.

POSSIBLE REASONS FOR DOUBT OR FEAR

Many people face fears regarding competitors when they externally roll out the Vivid Vision. Given the extremely personal nature of the Vivid Vision, there's a tendency to worry that someone might steal your ideas. And while that feeling is certainly real, in actuality, no one else has the ability to execute your ideas.

Remember, you're only showing them the final product; they have no idea how to get there. The Vivid Vision isn't your business plan, just your destination. And once you announce where you're going, you have staked out that territory. Should anyone else attempt to plant their flag there, it will only come off as derivative, as if that company doesn't have enough vision to chart its own course.

The other reason people often get nervous about this unveiling process is because they don't know a crucial element involved in it: the "how."

There's a certain vulnerability that comes with not having all the answers. It's difficult to stand in front of a room filled with people and make a bold announcement. It's even more difficult to do this without knowing the answer to the question, "How are you going to make that happen?"

Again, remember that the "how" is not your job. Omniscience is not a prerequisite for being the head of a company. You have people for that. If and when that question comes up during the external rollout, then answer it simply and confidently like this: "My team, in whom I have the utmost trust, will get it done, because that's the task I have charged them with."

REASONS FOR SHARING WITH THE WORLD

When you share your Vivid Vision with the world, the world comes to accept it. Sometimes, this happens very suddenly. People just wake up one day, and it's as if their blinders slip off. The world that you described to them, they can now see, clearly, right in front of their eyes. You have become like Henry Fonda who won over the other eleven men on the jury in the classic movie 12 *Angry Men*.

This change in perspective can trigger a chain reaction within and outside your organization. Inside, everybody begins to see and feel what you do. It prompts them to make decisions much more intuitively, understanding that they, too, have seen the promised land.

Outside the company, people look in and see that your organization functions as a single super-organism. They begin to realize that in three years, maybe you really will achieve that Big, Hairy, Audacious Goal. To that end, you'll want to walk certain core customers, like suppliers, through the Vivid Vision and the future of your company, so they don't randomly hear about the Big, Hairy, Audacious Goal. You want them to hear directly from you about the company's future.

When we were building 1-800-GOT-JUNK?, we sat down with the supplier who made all the blue boxes for the back of the trucks. We showed them what our company would look like three years out. He said, "I'm glad you told me. We do not have anywhere near that amount of trucks being ordered even to come to North America next year."

Our vision of what our future looked like rested upon his company being aware of our needs. For our Vivid Vision to come true, it was mandatory that we shared it with our supplier, so he could help us achieve the dream.

When you share the Vivid Vision with key people, like a supplier, they can plan accordingly, too. It may mean their needs change. Now, your Vivid Vision not only impacts your company, but it may cause a domino effect, prompting everyone connected to your business to scale up their own efforts to meet your expectations.

People don't want to work *for* exciting, inspiring companies; they want to work *with* them. If you're an exciting customer who talks about doubling your growth in three years, that will grab the attention of others, who will want to grow right alongside you. As a result, you're going to get more of their time and service—maybe even a better rate.

A DANCING GUY, JET PILOTS, AND BRICKLAYERS

Often, getting others to see your organization as you

see it is a matter of perseverance. An example of that is evident in a video that went viral, which I enjoy sharing with people as an illustration of the power of one person's ideas. It is from the Sasquatch! Music Festival from several years back. One guy danced by himself—not in a sad way. He seemed happy enough, but he was all alone.

He danced for about thirty seconds, while people stood around watching him. A minute later, he was still dancing, alone, as a crowd gathered on a huge grass hillside to watch. No one joined, but he kept dancing. After a while, another guy finally decided to join. Now, there were two guys dancing around, with people on the hillside watching. Then another guy joined, so there were three dancers.

Moments later, people ran down the hillside to join this little group of dancing guys. Thousands upon thousands of people danced around the guy who, just minutes before, danced alone.

A tipping point had occurred, and suddenly everyone's thinking changed.

Like the guy dancing alone, you will have to win others to your side with your Vivid Vision. Along the way, you may be challenged by others, possibly ridiculed.

There may be times when even people within your own building doubt the viability of the Vivid Vision. This, of course, is why it's so important to keep reading the document aloud and to keep sharing it with others outside the organization.

You will face obstacles as you work to make your Vivid Vision a reality, and the best way to overcome those obstacles is to align the company, as tightly as possible, to move forward as a single unit.

Think about jet pilots, like the Blue Angels, who fly as a team. At ridiculous speeds, in a sky with no demarcations or signage, these pilots weave in and out of various formations with deftness, beauty, and grace. How do they do it? They're perfectly aligned.

If these pilots didn't follow their maneuvers to the letter, a collision would be inevitable. The pilot not only must know exactly what his job is, but he has to know what the other guys are doing, as well. And just as important, if not more so, he has to trust that they will, in fact, do their jobs and do them perfectly. This is how you want your operation to run—smoothly and almost by instinct.

Especially in today's complex, fast-paced world, big shifts happen in the market all the time that change the economy and impact business. It's much easier to pivot and change how your business operates if your team is already aligned, which the Vivid Vision can really enhance. Getting people on the same page in the midst of a major pivot can be as unwieldy as trying to back a semi down a one-way alley. Or it can be as smooth as a couple of Blue Angels zigzagging across the empty sky, if everyone is aligned.

In our modern workplace, establishing and maintaining alignment is becoming more and more difficult. One major reason for this is off-site work where it's a challenge to keep remote employees aligned. The same is true of freelancers, independent contractors, part-time and temporary workers, and other essential players in your workforce.

It's important, therefore, that these people really understand what the big picture is and how they fit into it. There's an analogy that works well of a guy walking down the street who comes upon three guys making bricks. He asks the first guy, "What are you doing?"

And the first guy says, "I'm making bricks."

He asks the second guy, "What are you doing?"

And the second guy says, "I'm making these bricks to build a wall."

He asks the third guy, "What are you doing?"

And the third guy says, "I'm making these bricks to build the wall of a glorious cathedral that will be used for the worship of God."

Of those three guys, who do you think feels a greater alignment of purpose when he goes to work every morning? Yes, all of them are just making bricks, but the third guy understands *why* he's making bricks, and he understands the significance of those bricks.

Your people may not be building actual bricks, but you want them to understand the significance of their role in your company.

SAMPLE VIVID VISION:
BLUEGRACE LOGISTICS (2017)

The year is 2017 and we have reached three exceptional milestones as a team—our annual revenue is $500 million, we have 180 new members in our franchise family, and we remain 100% privately owned and self-financed. BlueGrace is VIBRANT and is regarded as "THE Place to Work." Our core belief is in the power of our people and a relentless pursuit of new ideas. Combine that with our commitment to deliver exceptional service, and we have hit a home run. These values are present in every facet of our company, bringing strength and integrity to our business that our competition can't touch. Our core values are not just lived; they are apparent to everyone who knows us. Our reach is global, and our system is located throughout North America. Things change rapidly—we adjust with little disruption and only utilize the best systems. Key leaders spend more time on strategy and execution than ever, and even in their absence nothing misses a beat.

BLUEGRACE HQ

Guests and employees alike can feel our energy before they walk through our front doors.

From the BlueGrace parking lot, they are greeted by our favorite music streaming outside, beckoning them into the lobby. Once inside, we deliver a wow experience through a beautiful, energetic space and a dynamic (and memorable!) person to greet our visitors. After being guided past the front office staff, the doors open and there they see—and feel—the heart and soul of BlueGrace.

Two hundred and fifty people are buzzing, smiling, and moving about, and that alone creates a surge of energy. The look is warm, fun, and modern throughout our space. We are now working in a completely refreshed, open, and unified environment and are all under one roof. Our walls have been transformed by displaying our most prized awards and our favorite quotes. Music fills the air, and employees curate the playlist. We have spaces in our office to provide for creativity, collaboration, and unwinding. Couches, bean bags, and even a relaxing outdoor space make sure our team is refreshed. We seldom see doors closed or blinds drawn anymore—the energy is CONTAGIOUS!

GREAT COMPANY. GREAT PEOPLE.

Our people make us who we are. Employees at BlueGrace are invested in making our company successful and share in our drive to be unstoppable in our marketplace. We are a leading employer in Tampa and are firmly entrenched as Tampa's BEST PLACE TO WORK. Our employees are outstanding—they feel valued and have crystal-clear roles and goals for their position, and a well-defined career plan. BlueGrace management takes the concept of "team" to a whole new level not only by committing to excellence in their own roles but by pledging to provide outstanding employee development. Our teams are empowered to cultivate greatness and are supported by BG to be intuitive, creative, and determined in all they do. Collaboration is everywhere—from meetings to the water cooler. We thrive on the buzz that these connections create. We feel like a family and only have "A" and "B" players working with us. Culture "misses" at BG have been quickly identified and replaced with absolute culture "HITS." Trust and morale are at an all-time high. We hear our teammates discussing ways to improve not only BG, but themselves, too. We now have a DREAM MANAGER—solely committed to making BG employees' personal dreams come true.

BRAND

BlueGrace is a world-class franchise system that specializes in shipping and logistics. In fact, we're more than that—our systems compete with any business of any size. We dominate every market we serve.

Because we consistently deliver excellence, we are intimidating to our competition and are embraced by employees, customers, and vendors.

Clients repeatedly say we make their life simpler, and they only wish they'd worked with BG sooner. They have close relationships with us; they trust us and see us as a true partner in the success of their business. They're constantly giving us referrals and testimonials and are thrilled to be included in our media interviews. Our clients love visiting our headquarters in Tampa, and travel from all over North America (and beyond) to see how we create "the BlueGrace magic."

MARKETING

Our dedicated media team is KILLING IT! Our PR efforts are run like a sales team, and they're pitching constantly. Media regularly turns to us as experts, and BlueGrace is written about frequently. We have had TV spots on all the major networks and mentions in the *Wall Street Journal*, *New York Times*, *Entrepreneur Magazine*, and *Forbes*. And we write a fantastic column in a leading franchise magazine and blog.

BlueGrace is now a full-service creative agency—each member of the team is an expert in their field. Because of the robust skill set of our internal team, our need to outsource has been reduced significantly. Because our marketing is a machine with LOTS of creative freedom, it creates incredible buzz among our customers and in the industry. We have positioned BG as the go-to source for B2B franchise expertise. Our efforts are thorough and transparent, and we track ROI on every project.

OPERATIONS

We have full integration of our CRM, billing, and shipping systems! Customer service has visibility to every area and has become a true one-stop shop. We review our service offerings annually to make sure we are staying ahead of the competition in value, pricing, and services. We have vibrant, full, and culturally "wow" BlueGrace offices in Chicago, Orlando, Tampa, and Baltimore—all promoting operational value through employee excellence.

FINANCE

Because our balance sheet is so healthy, we are still privately owned. The company is constantly building free cash flow, with little debt on our books, and our preferred lines with our banking partners have allowed for quick execution on acquisitions. We have completed the migration to our new ERP accounting software and have a formal FP&A department. BlueShip has been significantly updated and is offering seamless customer management—gone are the manual credit card transactions. The credit limits have been automated, and the interface is extraordinarily intuitive.

SALES

Our sales team of 75–100 is recognized in the industry as a best-in-class sales organization. We have customer onboarding down to a science and have an ongoing customer engagement model that maximizes long-term customer retention and eliminates churn. We are promoters of "the BG process," and we do not deviate from it. Our customer base, overall, is less transactional. Corporately, we are heavily weighted toward larger, repeat customers with predicated shipping patterns and needs. We are THRIVING and loving the success of doubling the business and then doubling it again.

FRANCHISE

We awarded more than 180 new BlueGrace franchises, are recognized as one of the best options in franchising, and are the overwhelmingly BEST choice within the transportation and logistics industry. Our new systems for identifying these people helped us accelerate the process with incredible accuracy and success. We have numerous instances where successful franchise owners have sold a franchise and monetized its value, and we have many franchise owners that own multiple units. We constantly obsess over the success of each franchise and are routinely rated "world-class" by our franchise system.

TECHNOLOGY

We have a clearly defined and budgeted technology plan with buy-in from stakeholders across the company. We are integrated via API in every possible situation, and because we have built a team of technology experts, our need to outsource is minimal. Our TMS capabilities on the BlueShip platform are widely recognized as robust, user-friendly, and feature-rich. This has driven and supported our sales process for clients of all sizes. We have perfected rapid customer engagement, onboarding, and integration processes. Our websites have evolved with industry-changing tools that drive business growth and customer interaction. We have won awards within the industry for innovation, simplicity, and design. Technology is considered a true core competency and differentiation point in our business.

RECRUITING AND TRAINING

BlueGrace has best-in-class training and is looked at by our competitors for the systems we have designed and implemented. Away from the office, BlueGrace employees are constantly telling their family and peers about their life at work. They're so happy they work with BG, that over 50% of our new hires come from employee referrals. Because BlueGrace provides such a supportive and engaging work environment, the supply of exceptionally qualified candidates always exceeds our demand.

LEGAL

We have built a reputation for three things: (1) being tremendously strong in our field, (2) the quality of our work, and (3) fast legal service. Our legal team has grown to support our increased need for sound guidance, and we are known as being very easy to work with and for providing excellent advice. We are an educational resource for the entire BlueGrace system and help the BG family learn the best practices and methods for protecting their interests.

COMMITMENT TO COMMUNITY

Two dedicated BlueGrace team members are making our commitment to community a wild success. One specializes in external efforts, like philanthropy and event planning; the other focuses on internal culture and health—namely, the BG wellness programs and employee personal success. We're helping our employees build their bucket lists and are helping them cross off items, too. BlueGrace philanthropy is unmatched, and we are known for being extremely generous with both financial aid and active involvement through our "Giving Grace" program. We have extended our "Cats versus Dogs" program throughout the nation and now supply over 150,000 pounds of food to shelter animals across the United States.

PART FOUR

HOW TO MAKE IT COME TRUE

CHAPTER 9

REVERSE ENGINEERING

THREE YEARS CAN FEEL like an eternity. Some days, you may feel like the three-year span of the Vivid Vision is so far away that you can't even consider it. In those moments, you may wonder, *"How do I even get started on something so massive and so distant?"*

During all of these moments, it's easy to become overwhelmed, weighted down by a discouraging sense that there's just too much to accomplish and not enough time.

No matter which source of dread you experience, the solution is the same: take it one small step at a time. As the saying goes, Rome wasn't built in a day.

See your grand ambition not so much as a single entity but as dozens of smaller entities linked together to form something singular.

Realize that every sentence in your Vivid Vision is a goal in and of itself. And to bring about each sentence, a certain number of projects will need to be performed in a certain order. Looking at one individual project is certainly much less daunting than accomplishing the goal of the whole sentence, and far, far less intimidating than the entirety of your three-year vision.

By breaking down your goals into bite-sized pieces, you will be able to overcome each obstacle as it arises and finalize each necessary project along the journey.

Recall the home that we're building. You begin with the foundation and build upward from there. There is groundwork that must be laid if you're going to accomplish your BHAG, and the projects that behave as that foundation are your starting point.

Begin by looking at the initiatives tied to one of these three main areas: core purpose, core values, or BHAG. Make sure your team understands and really feels these initiatives.

Next, look to your human resources to ensure that the human element of your operation is aligned and running smoothly. You need every system related to people-training, onboarding, recruiting, interviewing, selecting and hiring talent, keeping people happy, and eliminating bad apples to work well.

Next, you want to ensure that strategic thinking systems are working, and that all meetings are being run productively and efficiently.

REVERSE ENGINEERING

The key to crossing the chasm between today and three years from now is by starting three years from now and working backward through time. *Huh?* That may sound strange, but this is the reverse-engineering process. Reverse engineering essentially looks at the finished state of a goal, and then you work backward from the end point to where you are now to determine the steps you need to take to get to the future.

Imagine planning a dinner party. You think about what time people should sit down to eat, and based on that calculation, you determine what time the food should come out of the oven. When you know what time the food should come out, then you can figure out when the food needs to go in.

This is reverse engineering.

So, for your own BHAG, consider all the different products that you're going to need, and then think about when the different components of it need to be put together. If they are being put together, then think about in what order that must happen—consider when you'll need to order the materials, for example, or line up the subtrades, or whatever. Once you have the plan laid out, you just execute it going forward.

People tend to get seduced by the big, shiny object. They look at something that seems exciting and get distracted by that, rather than understanding the gestational nature of the process that may be required. To return to the metaphor, there's nothing sexy about putting down the foundation; it's much more enticing to think about putting the red knobs on the Wolf stove. But working backward requires that those knobs be among the final tasks undertaken.

Another setback on the road to accomplishing your three-year plan is the coming-back-to-Earth that can happen after the retreat is over and you're back in your office and everything literally returns to business as usual. It's possible to become discouraged. This is one of the reasons to pull out the document on a regular basis and read it. Get inspired. The other solution is, again, breaking the big goal down into more manageable pieces.

CONCEIVE, BELIEVE, AND ACHIEVE

The Vivid Vision does not have to be the only instrument designed to inspire your team. I also have clients who have built a "Can You Imagine?" wall, which is a creative way to engage more people, as the Vivid Vision is the singular vision of the organization's top official.

When people are reading the Vivid Vision, they might say, "Yeah, that's great, but I had a couple of ideas, too." Their ideas may not be right for the Vivid Vision, but they can be incorporated into an inspirational image of what the future of the company may look like. The way to do that is to post those ideas on a wall. It's that simple. You post people's inspirational goals up on the wall, goals that they can imagine happening in the future. And just as with the Vivid Vision, you cross those things off as each is completed.

One of the boldest goals, for instance, that we posted on our wall at 1-800-GOT-JUNK? read, "Can you imagine getting our brand name on the side of a Starbucks cup?" Another was, "Can you imagine our company being studied at Harvard Business School?"

Both of those things did, in fact, happen.

You'll notice that those statements aren't just inspirational thoughts but real goals. You want concrete actions that can be achieved and crossed off. You want what you write to be bold and inspirational, but you also want these sentences to be realistic enough that your employees can figure out a way to make them come true.

This activity is not only good for company morale, but it helps to anchor the Vivid Vision, as people begin to realize, "Wow, if we can make *this* goal happen, maybe that Big, Hairy, Audacious Goal is also achievable."

MAINTAINING THE VISION

THE VIVID VISION is a tool, like a shovel. And just as a shovel can't dig a hole unless you pick it up and use it, the Vivid Vision, likewise, has to be used to be effective. You can't just write it, throw it in a drawer, and hope that your Vivid Vision becomes a reality.

Part of using the Vivid Vision means revisiting it again and again.

When people see tangible progress being made, it sparks a wave of encouragement throughout the organization. Just as the "Can You Imagine" wall allows employees to see goals being accomplished, when you mark up the Vivid Vision, noting which goals have been met and which projects are currently in progress, the document becomes a visual barometer of progress.

I recommend revisiting the Vivid Vision every quarter as an organization. And when you read through the document, highlight in green each item that's been achieved, and then highlight in yellow the items currently in progress. You'll find that every few months, the document becomes more colorful and more alive, as you note every passing milestone.

As you mark off completed tasks, you'll move on to assign new ones as the long three-year process slowly reveals itself to you. That, too, is a source of inspiration. Employees appreciate challenges, particularly challenges that have a visible purpose.

There's a few different ways to incorporate the Vivid Vision into a meeting agenda or to ensure that the message of the document is hammered home to your team. Some clients insist that one paragraph of their Vivid Vision must be read at every meeting that involves three or more people. Another client begins every strategic planning meeting by going over the document.

This type of repetition is a good thing. It provides

everyone on your team with the same mindset, as if everyone is watching the same scene of Julie Andrews singing in the meadow from *The Sound of Music*. And that is the underlying concept of the Vivid Vision: When everyone can see what the CEO can see, they will figure out a way to make that dream for the future come true.

You'll likely be tempted to constantly tweak the document or course-correct as you go along, especially when you see that things happen that you didn't expect or intend. The reality is you will probably have to make some minor course corrections as you go.

It's like putting a rocket into orbit—it's not a straight line. You have to adjust for various unaccounted-for factors that arise along the way. But the key thing is that you're always pointed in the same direction. You don't want to change the items on the Vivid Vision during the three-year period unless there has been some massive, seismic shift in your industry or in the world.

What happens when you hit the end of the three-year period? What does success, actually, look like? At the end of the day, most people will wonder, *"Well, there's a bunch of stuff on our Vivid Vision that didn't turn out to be true. So does that mean we've failed?"*

The answer: Absolutely not!

Crossing items off the list isn't the only metric by which you can or should measure your success.

One of the purposes of the Vivid Vision is to create alignment on your team. At the end of the three years, you should consider how well-aligned your team became. How engaged were they? Are people more clear on their duties and responsibilities than they were before you released the Vivid Vision? How much harmony was created inside the office when projects were being planned and picked out?

What you will see is that engagement levels go way up and conflict goes down when you have a Vivid Vision that everyone is aligned toward achieving. People focus more, and they work harder to get more done. And that momentum creates more momentum for your company.

As a result, you will see more growth.

My contention has always been that companies that execute this plan will double their revenue in three years or less. They will get a minimum of 26% growth for three years in a row, which equates to double. And that—the engagement, productivity, profit, and growth—is really a better measuring stick than whether or not every item on the list was highlighted in green.

When workers within an organization are making decisions with the same intuition as their leader, that is a hallmark of success. That is one of the reasons you're training people to be leaders in the first place. Your job as the CEO is to align and inspire everyone and then get out of the way and let them run.

When the guy making bricks understands that he's really building a cathedral, he sees greater purpose in his work. He sees how he is connected to something larger than himself. That imbues his work with meaning and shows him his value within the organization.

This sense of meaning and purpose is one of the most fulfilling outcomes of the Vivid Vision experience.

When it comes time to craft the next Vivid Vision, your confidence level will be exponentially higher, knowing that your team has the potential to gel. You can dream even bigger, feeling more secure in the knowledge that your team has already risen to the challenge and that they're already well-aligned, ready to tackle the next set of challenges.

And when it's time to begin work on that next document, you'll find you can envision in greater detail. The descriptions are more focused because you'll have the experiential knowledge you acquired the first time around, and you'll apply what you have learned to this new document. More importantly, your employees will grasp the concepts much more easily and align faster.

In fact, employees will begin to look ahead and wonder what the next Vivid Vision will encompass. And they'll wonder when the next Vivid Vision will begin.

The answer to that last question is two to three months in advance. You read that right. You have to get an early jump on it.

SUBSEQUENT VIVID VISIONS

FOR MY SECOND VIVID VISION. I set loftier goals for my company. When it comes time to write your second Vivid Vision—and that time will come sooner than you expect—the only difference from your first document is in magnitude.

Like last time, you'll want to find a serene setting and follow the same procedures as your first Vivid Vision experience. I wrote my second Vivid Vision inspired by the lake and mountains I overlooked at my chalet in Whistler—the chalet I included as part of my BHAG in my first Vivid Vision.

My next Vivid Vision—the fourth—I plan to write at my golf course. There's a back patio where I can enjoy a beautiful view of the course. It's elegant and feels very inspiring. And that is all you need. You do not have to take a journey or be in a remote place—you could do it in the lobby of a historic hotel in the city or at any favorite location in which you feel inspired.

My focus for this version was to raise my game as a speaker and to get my first book launched. In terms of speaking engagements, I envisioned increasing the size of my speaking fees, and I saw myself choosing larger and more prestigious venues to speak at. I imagined doing conferences for *Forbes*, *Fortune*, *Inc.*, and other branded events run by the big business magazines.

I employed the same writer to make the words come to life, and I started using more professional brand imagery on this second Vivid Vision. I got rid of the cartoons, which I felt diminished and cheapened the document. But that was my personal feeling, and you can decide for yourself, of course, what you want yours to look like.

Once you have composed your Vivid Vision, you'll want to break down the goals in terms of a time frame, the same as you did in your first version. What do you hope to accomplish by the end of the first quarter? What about the end of the second and third quarters? What foundation do you hope to have laid by the end of the first year? What about the second year?

As my own CEO, I only concerned myself with what the finish line looked like. If I had been operating a large organization, I would have delegated the operational task of the "how," of getting there, to my employees. At that time, the operations were mine alone to carry out. But rather than wear two hats simultaneously, I first played the role of CEO, envisioning the big picture. Once that was in place, I focused on how to implement it.

As a result of this second version, I began to see with greater clarity which opportunities were essential to my goals and which were off course. In fact, decisions that I might have struggled with resolved themselves for the most part. For instance, I had a potential client with whom I enjoyed speaking on the phone, but I knew I would not enjoy coaching him. This person wasn't in my sweet spot and wasn't the caliber of client I was aiming for.

I knew I wouldn't engage passionately with him, so I suggested one of my associates would be a better coach. It turned out to be mutually beneficial for both of them, and for me since the job wasn't consistent with my three-year goals. But if I hadn't clearly spelled out those goals or charted my course, I may have taken on that client simply for the money. And money is something that takes a lot of people off course, since it's very lucrative in the short run.

The idea for the second and subsequent documents is to build off of the original Vivid Vision. It's like adding a new wing to your house, or updating the bathrooms and cabinets, or giving it a new paint job. You're not starting from the ground up; rather, you just keep moving in the direction that you already started. That will mean there is no point in writing down aspects of your business that you envisioned and later implemented, because now they already exist.

BENEFITS BIG AND SMALL

THE POSITIVE EFFECTS of sharing the Vivid Vision within the organization is only a beginning. As I mentioned earlier, you'll reap many benefits from your Vivid Vision when you share it with people outside of your organization, too. Everyone you do business with—everyone who touches or is touched by your business—will feel the same passion about the future you're building toward that you do.

When your suppliers, for example, gain a better understanding of exactly what your company is on the road to becoming, they can figure out their role in the endeavor. It might mean scaling up to meet your demands, like the supplier I mentioned in a previous chapter. Or it may mean they have to streamline some aspect of their operation to supply you faster, as they attempt to keep your business.

And as I said before, they may give you better pricing, as they start to see you as a larger company that will represent a greater share of their profits. They might even decide to lock you in by offering you better rates for a longer period of time. And you may also find that you get better, faster, and more responsive service from them.

Your customers, too, will be more excited about the future. If you're selling a product, they'll have the reassurance that you've thought through what those products will look like even three years out, and they will be excited about what the future brings in terms of new improvements. If, on the other hand, you provide a service, your customers will be reassured by the fact that they're signing up for something that is built to last, not just a fly-by-night operation. This may bode well for securing longer-term contracts.

Of course, as a customer, you are never just buying a product or service. What you're really doing is entering into a relationship. This is why branding is so important. You want your reputation as a company to be a strong one. This will help you make new relationships, while maintaining current ones.

The last thing you want is to plan for the future by crossing your fingers and hoping your current customers will keep choosing to do business with you. Isn't it better to plan with the certainty of your customers' loyalty? I sure think so. And it's a certainty that the Vivid Vision helps establish.

STABILITY

Some years ago, I was looking to buy a car. I chose a Saab. The next thing I knew, the company declared bankruptcy. "Great," I thought. "Now, I'm stuck with a car without a company behind it."

It wasn't very reassuring.

It's important that customers feel good about your company and about where it's going. You will find that customers will make buying decisions based on what the company is going to look like in the future. It's your job to share that information with them.

Volatility is a frightening proposition in any relationship, but when it comes to a business relationship, it can be a deal breaker. You want to know that anyone you shake hands with has enough stability that you feel safe putting your trust in that person.

If you are a $4 million company today, and that is all your customers see about you, then you're not helping yourself or them. They need to see you as the $10 million company you will be three years from now. That will both better inform their decisions and increase your appeal as a company.

Suppliers and customers, of course, are making investments in your company, but then there are bankers, financiers, venture capitalists, or maybe shareholders, who are literally investing in your company. These people are already looking three years into the future. If you don't share your Vivid Vision of what your company will look like with them, they'll have to rely on their own imagination as to what your company will look like.

Their imagination doesn't help you.

Years ago, one of my clients was trying to get a bank loan. They actually took their Vivid Vision document into the bank and walked the banker through it, looking three years into the future. Afterward, the banker looked up and said, "Wow, I finally understand your company and where you're going. I never really understood it from the business plan and your spread-sheets, but now I get it."

THE "WOW" FACTOR

There is a synergy that happens when people outside of the company start getting excited about you. The outside excitement inspires everyone inside the walls. It makes your employees feel like they're part of something bigger. When other people are talking about your company, the engagement within the company rises. It makes your company more attractive to potential new employees, as well.

The "wow" factor is priceless for a brand.

As I mentioned earlier, your Vivid Vision will also have the added benefit of scaring away the wrong potential recruits. The more clearly that would-be employees see what your company is about, the more they can gauge whether they're a good fit for it. It's important, then, that the Vivid Vision be a part of the interviewing and recruiting process. If a potential hire doesn't share in your vision, you can suss that out ahead of time, rather than making a costly decision in hiring that person.

And if you lose people, like my client who lost 15% of

his team when he rolled out his Vivid Vision, that's really OK. The people who stay are the ones on board with the direction of the company, the ones who accept their roles in bringing about the document's goals.

You want to build momentum with your Vivid Vision, and you need people engaged and committed to do this. Momentum is a critical factor in any organization. Just as success breeds success, positive energy generates more positive energy. The flip side of that, of course, is that negative energy spawns more negative energy.

The media, both professional and social, is yet another source to leverage in sharing your Vivid Vision. Journalists will write about you, telling your story to their readers. The better they understand you, the more accurate the story told to the public will be. And that story, to reiterate, is not what you, as a company, are right now; it is who you are three years from now. What you're doing right now may not be newsworthy, but what you're doing three years from now—assuming your BHAG is big and hairy and audacious enough—is.

VALIDATION

You need the media to buy in to the Vivid Vision if you want others to buy in to it. The imprimatur of the media is necessary, as it carries a watchdog function, filtering out truth from fiction and reality from fantasy. The more that you can convince the people within the media of what your future looks like, the more you'll convince the greater public.

There is a validation you get when people read about your company in a newspaper or magazine. There is a social proof that makes legitimate what you're doing that you can't get by having people read your marketing materials or business plans.

You need objective, third-party confirmation.

When the media writes about companies, they often ask questions based on whatever it is that is right in front of them at that moment. They ask details about the company's current condition and climate. A Vivid Vision changes the shape of your message, giving the media something else to talk about that is more inspiring. It allows you to stand out from the crowd because everyone else the media is writing about is focused on what they look like today.

As a species, we have a fascination with novelty. We

want to see new things. We were blessed with the gift of imagination that we may create original things. That inspires and excites us. Naturally, this is the stuff that people want to read about. Journalists, knowing this, are eager to share stories about the "next big thing."

Furthermore, when the media reinforces the message you're telling the world about your company's future, the prophecy is more likely to become self-fulfilling. If you want to be seen and regarded as a $10 million company, you need others to believe that that is what you are, and when that's what people are reading and hearing about you, they respond accordingly.

If you believe that not all publicity is good publicity, then you realize that the media is a two-edged sword. Yes, it can do wonders for your image in the public eye—assuming you have leveraged it to see you as you see yourself. But if you don't give them that glimpse three years into the future, what are they left to talk about other than what you are right at this moment? A mere $4 million company. Then, they're left to speculate about what your future holds.

As I am fond of saying, in the absence of facts, people make up their own.

Once the media has disseminated your vision, your marketing department can leverage that fact. Marketing departments love sound bites and blurbs. Now that you have the stamp of approval from traditional forms of media, whether it be print, broadcast, or digital, you can take that and leverage it in the ever-expanding realm of social media.

Now, you can take the link to that story and tweet it: "Look what the *NY Times* is saying about us." You can post the video of an interview you did with a local news station on your Facebook page. You can leverage all the tools of social media to bombard the online world with the content that you want it to be aware of.

You are the master of your brand, and if you want others to see you as the $10 million company you will be in three years, rather than as the $4 million company you are today, that power is literally in the palm of your hands.

SAMPLE VIVID VISION:
FISH MARKETING (2017)

"It's impossible to reach your destination if you don't know where you're going."

– DOUG FISH

OUR MISSION

We are committed to providing a healthy, nurturing, and dynamic work environment for our employees and strategic, creative, and effective marketing campaigns that help our clients grow.

OUR CORE VALUES

Trust, honesty, and integrity are our highest values. We work hard and play hard. We respect each other and our clients.

OUR CULTURE

Every employee is thoroughly engaged and understands how his or her role fits in the big picture. We trust each other implicitly and hold each other accountable for excellent work, meeting deadlines and hitting budgets. Our staff enjoys hanging out with each other, and we regularly devote company time to socializing and fun. We consistently average 7.0+ in job satisfaction surveys. Employees are constantly making suggestions on how to improve our culture and what we do.

Our PTO schedule is as good as any in Portland, providing a minimum of four weeks of PTO plus nine holidays per year:

- 0–3 Years: 4 Weeks
- 3–10 Years: 5 Weeks
- 10+ Years: 6 Weeks

OUR OFFICES

Our offices encompass the entire sixth floor of the Olympic Mills Commerce Center. Our teams are clustered in open areas near breakout rooms where meetings and conversations take place frequently. We have two kitchen areas and three lounge areas where employees can relax, eat, and converse. When visitors come to our office, they are impressed and want to work in a space like ours.

OUR DEPARTMENTS

Client Services—Responsible for client relationships, goals, budgets, and efficiencies that lead to profitability for the agency and growth for clients.

Digital—Produces best-in-class solutions for our clients and stays abreast of the latest developments in interactive marketing.

Creative—Delivers compelling, strategic copy, design, and video for all client campaigns.

Media—Provides effective, efficient media buys; stays on top of the latest trends in online and traditional media; shares software and ratings tools with MBT.

Finance and Administration—Generates client billing by the tenth of every month and timely financial metrics to assess monthly agency performance.

Public Affairs—Oversees public affairs and marketing work and manages relationships for government, nonprofit, and corporate clients.

MANAGEMENT STRUCTURE

We have twenty-eight full-time employees and utilize several freelancers for creative and digital work on an as-needed basis.

Our management team includes a VP of Operations, VP of Client Services, VP of Public Affairs, Director of Business Development, Digital Director, Creative

Director, and Controller. No manager has more than six direct reports. The VP of Operations oversees finance, creative, digital, media, and administration; the remainder of the management team reports to the President.

REGULARLY SCHEDULED MEETINGS

Weekly—We hold production meetings with creative, digital, and account teams to review current projects and ensure smooth workflow. Employees have weekly one-on-one meetings with their managers to discuss goals, best practices, areas for coaching, and opportunities to help in reaching goals.

Monthly—The management team and each department meets monthly to review performance, discuss opportunities, solve issues, and make decisions that will improve outcomes.

Quarterly—All-staff meetings are held quarterly to review the Vivid Vision, report on financial metrics, discuss new initiatives, and reward outstanding performances.

Annually—In the fall, the management team conducts a two-day, offsite planning retreat to set objectives and strategies for the coming year.

OUR CLIENTS

Our clients are a mix of small- to mid-sized companies, governmental agencies, and nonprofit organizations.

Our smallest clients generate a minimum of $24,000 in gross income. All of our clients believe we are helping them achieve their business goals and see us as a trusted advisor, not a vendor.

Our clients' businesses are growing, and their budgets are also growing by an average of 10% per year. No single client accounts for more than 20% of our gross income.

We only handle project work that is a strategic fit.

PROJECT CRITERIA

· Leads to ongoing, sustainable work
· Within a business category we seek to gain expertise in
· Fills a revenue or utilization gap caused by seasonal slowdowns
· For a large client that we seek to gain a foothold with
· For a pro bono client we agree to support

Pro bono clients receive a 10% discount on all fee-based work and are selected by the management team. Very few clients leave because they are unhappy. Annually, we lose less than 10% of prior year revenue to client attrition.

NEW BUSINESS

We strive for new clients who offer ongoing, sustainable revenue. New business leads come from referrals, Google search, and sales outreach in categories where we have a strategic advantage. We have a strict set of criteria for determining which accounts to pursue. A Director of Business Development oversees marketing and sales and works closely with the management team to generate 25% revenue growth from new clients.

PARTNERS

We share offices and overhead expenses with MBT Marketing. We occasionally collaborate on new business pitches and frequently share ideas and best practices. Client conflicts are minimal and kept in check by strict nondisclosure agreements signed by all employees from both agencies.

TECHNOLOGY

We pride ourselves on utilizing the latest technologies to constantly improve efficiency. We commonly use video conferencing when conducting meetings with clients outside the office.

THE NUMBERS

In 2017, we generated $4 million in gross income on $10 million in sales.

Our new profit margin was 23%.

We have 28 full-time employees (FTE).

Our income per FTE is $12,000/month.

We consistently average 120 billable hours/FTE/month.

We pay annual bonuses, plus 1–10% pay increases based on performance. All employees understand exactly what is expected of them to meet, exceed, or blow away their individual goals in order to earn a raise. Our salaries meet or exceed the average for comparable positions in the Portland market, based on Portland Ad Federation's biannual salary survey.

PART FIVE

APPLYING VIVID VISION TO YOUR PERSONAL LIFE

YOUR PERSONAL JOURNEY

AS HUMANS, we hold the past and the future in our thoughts even as we live in the present. Each informs our decisions and guides our actions. Now that you've transported three years into the future and looked at every aspect of your business, what about the other dimensions of your life?

Is it possible to lean out into the future and examine your personal life?

The answer is yes.

As humans, we don't really think about what we want

our lives to look like down the road. Instead, we tend to take it as it comes, reacting, rather than being proactive. The purpose of the personal Vivid Vision, and the sharing and rereading of it with family and friends, is to live a more conscious life.

Living consciously allows us to perceive time more acutely by setting large goals and achieving them one action at a time, each day. We imbue our lives with greater meaning when our decisions are not just frivolous coin flips, but rather, well-strategized play calls.

You can create a personal Vivid Vision. You can even create one for your family. In my personal Vivid Vision, I see the kind of husband I want to be, the kind of father I want to be, and the kind of man I want to be.

Once again, you want to describe everything you see as you look around—only now you're looking around your home, rather than your office. And once again, this is not the time to think about *how* you will get there, only *that* you will get there. Aim high. You know you're going to work hard to accomplish what you set out to do, so why not make it a worthy cause?

Remember that you will start at that future point and work back from there—reverse engineering your life. If you don't have a vision of what you want your future self to look like, then how do you make decisions? It's like driving—if you don't know where you're going, you're just wasting fuel. If you don't have a plan, you're living from day to day or moment to moment. You wouldn't do that with your business, so why do it with the rest of your life?

Don't get me wrong, there's something enjoyable and important about living in the moment. And, naturally, there's a place for that; it's just not how you want to live every moment of the day. That leads to a sloppy and haphazard existence.

You need to clearly articulate the BHAGs in your personal life. Wishy-washy or vague won't work. For example, if your plan involved losing weight, you don't want a statement that says, "I will be thinner," or "I will be able to wear that new bathing suit." That level of opacity would be useless in business, and it's useless here. You need to be precise with goals quantitative in nature, such as: "I will lose forty-four pounds."

You need that level of precision. Precision establishes the projects you must accomplish along the way, and just like in your Vivid Vision for your business, you'll highlight in green the achievements you make. One first-year goal, for instance, might be to lose half the weight: twenty-two pounds. Now, when you review your personal Vivid Vision at quarterly intervals, you can mark that item as having been accomplished. (Weight loss probably is not the best example in this situation, as it is something that can fluctuate up and down, but you get the principle.)

A good decision demands precision. Knowing your goals with exactitude will inform your day-to-day decisions like, "Can I eat that bag of chips?" Without a crystal-clear goal, you don't know how to answer that question. And without certainty about that answer, you're probably going to eat those chips.

That level of precision is why I recommend looking three years ahead instead of twenty. Anything that far into the future comes with the built-in excuse of ignoring it. After all, what does that bag of chips mean in the course of two decades? Three years is the magic number. It gives you time to accomplish something big, which may require trial and error, or it gives you time to go down some rabbit holes even if they don't pan out.

THE FIVE F'S: FITNESS, FAITH, FINANCE, FAMILY, AND FRIENDS

The personal Vivid Vision is a little different than the one you use in a business environment. This one doesn't directly affect others. Your personal document will function more as a sort of contract with your friends and family. And just as you internally rolled out your business Vivid Vision, you'll want to share your personal one with the people in your life.

These people will be involved in helping you to realize your vision. They'll remind you about it, encourage you, and hopefully, hold you accountable. They might even incorporate aspects of your Vivid Vision into their own lives.

I have a friend who read in mine that I wanted to do more hiking and running (I worded it with more precision, of course), so every week I saw an email from him pop up asking if I wanted to go for a hike.

If you don't share these components with people, how can they really help you? How can they be sensitive to your needs? If you want to lose weight and they know that, they can help make that easier for you, like forgoing showing up on your doorstep with pizza.

The truth is, it is hard to accomplish big things on your own. Humans aren't wired that way. So think of the people in your life as your teammates. With a support group that believes in your cause, the sky becomes the limit for what you can accomplish.

With your company, you lean out into the future and describe what you see by exploring every business department—finance, marketing, IT, and so on. Your personal life is also departmentalized, if not quite as formally. These categories compose what I call the 5 F's: *Fitness, Faith, Finance, Family, and Friends.*

In each of these important aspects of your life, gaze three years out and begin by clearly describing every detail of what you see.

Fitness. How is your appearance different than it is today? Physically, what shape are you in? Peek into the medicine cabinet. How healthy are you?

You have three whole years to make your fitness goals happen, and in that time, you can improve your diet, get more exercise, take up a new sport or activity, get more rest, reduce stress, limit alcohol consumption, and adopt a healthier lifestyle. When you lean out into the future, the person you see reflected in the mirror should be a person who has spent three dedicated years waiting for that very day.

Faith. What does your spiritual life look like three years from now? Regardless of your faith, or lack thereof, there is an internal aspect of yourself that needs nurturing, particularly as you age and take steps closer to your death. Is the person in the mirror a reflective being or an automaton mindlessly going through this life? If you have taken the time and effort to vividly visualize your life, chances are you're the former. So how do you see yourself being even more reflective in your future? What does that look like to you?

Finance. What strides have you made as you look at your bank book? Again, be specific with your goals—have definitive figures you're looking at. You will work out the means of getting there later, but you need to first have a destination in mind. Know where you want to be in your career three years from today. Once you know where that place is, you can reverse engineer your way step-by-step.

Family. Now, look at your family. Dare to envision what is possible, knowing that your destiny is in your own hands even as it involves connections with others. What does your relationship with your spouse look like? Have you grown closer? Do you have more shared interests? Is there forgiveness for offenses? Are you a better life partner in three years than you are now? Ask yourself what your ideal relationship looks like, knowing that you'll soon work to make that happen.

If you're a parent, where do you see your relationship with your children in three years? No relationship in your life is as in flux as that between you and your children. Children develop so rapidly. They're filled with hormones that confuse them. And they're trying hard to navigate a world in which they're often pulled between friends and parents, and sometimes even between parents. Not only that, but your role as a parent evolves as they grow, as you work to raise them into self-sufficient adults.

Other important relationships to consider are those with your parents and siblings. As your parents age, you will take on new responsibilities, and that will likely affect the interactions you have with your siblings.

Friends. And what about your friends? Are you the kind of friend whom you would want to have? Do you see yourself as growing your network in your future life or simply growing ever closer to the friends you already have? Friendships require upkeep and commitment, and grow stronger or fade out depending on decisions you make. If you're conscious of these choices and take efforts to be a good friend, your relationships will last.

The difference between your business life and your

personal life is free time. Hopefully, you won't have free time at work. That would be unproductive and inefficient, but in our personal lives free time is a source of pleasure and possibility.

It's truly surprising how many moments actually go unaccounted for over the course of three consciously lived years. And if you're not treating that time as a valuable component of a master plan, you're more likely to waste that time. That's because it's not functioning as the canvas upon which the future is painted.

The personal Vivid Vision has its own form of self-fulfilling prophecy woven into its fabric. For starters, it acts as something of a contract with oneself. We make an implicit deal with ourselves to deliver the future that we envision.

Another way in which writing the Vivid Vision helps is that it fixes our gaze along the path we want to go. We only write down positive things about our future selves. These are our noblest goals. After all, why would we aim to be fatter, lousier, poorer, or anything else emblematic of backsliding? We write down positive traits about ourselves, and the very act of doing so plants those seeds in our minds, and we begin to feel and act accordingly because we walk in the direction in which we look.

One technique that should help you make better and more efficient use of your time is to ask yourself, "If I had one extra day each week, how would I spend it?"

When I ask myself this question, I have a list of activities that I would do on those eight days each week. My list includes spending more time with my wife, more time with my kids, hanging out with friends, going out for brunch, and reading books.

Once I identified what I *would* do with that hypothetical extra time, I built goals around them. I found time that already existed on the calendar, then blocked off certain weekends to get out of town with my wife, certain days to do things with my kids, and some days just to curl up with a good book. Without my Vivid Vision, I would have spent those days finding stuff to stay busy, but that stuff wouldn't have been in pursuit of bettering the Five F's of my future.

A VISION FOR YOUR FAMILY

HAVE YOU EVER WONDERED what your family will be like in three years? It's not a far-out idea. We all consider the future; usually we think about it in terms of what it will cost to send the kids to a certain school, if it will be feasible to move into a bigger house, or other practical decisions that we all face as families.

Do you think you and your spouse or partner share the same view of the future? What if you don't?

If you would never dare to be thoughtless in thinking about the future of your business, then why would you be cavalier about the future of your family? Why would you risk making the family journey without designing what you want your family life to be like?

In applying the Vivid Vision to your family life, you want to look closer than just the surface economic issues that will affect your major purchasing decisions, such as increased school tuition, or buying a new car or home.

So, for instance, what are the things that your family values? What sorts of activities will you do as a family? What will your vacations look and feel like? What is your day-to-day home life like? How would others describe you as a father? As a husband? As a friend? If someone was writing about you in a book, how would you be described?

It is a little bit like the movie *Citizen Kane*, in which Kane's legacy is discovered through the people who knew him. If your story were to be told facet by facet through the eyes of others, what would it look like? Imagine what you would want them to see, and reverse engineer your life to look like that.

If you're raising a child or children as a couple, it's important that you and your spouse are both on the same page. It's exactly the same as having two cofounders of a company who share in the creation of a Vivid Vision. I've had people write Vivid Vision statements centering around relationships with ex-wives or ex-husbands. They've worked together and stayed committed to building a strong relationship with their ex for the sake of the children. As a result, I have seen people survive very bitter divorces and come out on the other end having a very, very strong relationship with their ex.

The partners or spouses in the relationship basically act as CO-CEOS. As such, both individuals need to be involved in the writing process. But this doesn't mean that the document is written jointly. Writing as a team might sound like a good idea, but it can become a compromised vision or can be subconsciously shaped or driven more by one partner than the other.

Go to separate spaces where neither person is likely to be influenced by the other. Daydream as you would for yourself, and jot your ideas down as they come. Later, the two of you will come together and merge your visions into one—much like you did when you first got married. Only this time you're spelling details of the future out very clearly.

The ideal time to write the Vivid Vision is during a vacation, for the same reasons that a retreat is the best time to write the document for your business. A new year is another good time to craft the Vivid Vision, as most people intently consider and think about where they want their lives to go.

Unlike the business version, however, this Vivid Vision need only be about two or three pages, at most. I have seen much longer and more detailed ones, though, where people delve deeper into their activities and their feelings.

This version of the Vivid Vision makes an ideal precursor to a vision board, which will serve to illuminate the words in the document. Once you craft the Vivid Vision for yourself, it becomes very easy to find photos that can represent each sentence. You may find a photo that represents you as a loving husband. You may find another photo that represents you as a caring father. You may find another one that has you as an active individual. And you may find photos that represent each of your favorite sports.

The point is that it's easy to construct an image from each sentence within the document. And that vision board should be posted in your office, your home, or anywhere you can continually look at it for inspiration and motivation. This is something each child may enjoy creating, as well.

VISION BECOMES REALITY

BY TAKING the business concept of the Vivid Vision and adapting it to your family, you will find that your friends will want to spend more time with you because you are becoming a better person. You'll attract new people into your life, people who will be motivated to help you, who are inspired by you, and who are excited to be around you. And because of all those positive relationships, you will feel better. There are benefits that come from this that are actually similar to the benefits of having a company.

If you don't know where you are going, any road will take you there, as the Cheshire Cat from *Alice in Wonderland* explained. We only get one life. We only get one chance to build a great company. We only get one shot to do well in our careers.

Simply waking up every day and working hard or busying yourself is not necessarily going to be the most effective path or give you the best results. By using the Vivid Vision, you're going to have better success. You're going to have better luck. You're going to have more fun. You'll have everyone conspiring to help you. Additionally, it's a lot easier to get to the result you want when you know what that result is.

And it's easier to get where you want to go if you know what the destination is.

Recall the scene from *The Sound of Music.* If, as the writer of the film, you saw that scene in your head, how would you explain it in such a way that a director and a producer would also see it and that a cast and crew could re-create it? Is that not exactly what you're trying to do with your business?

You have a goal in mind of what you want to be in three years. How are you going to explain it in such a way that your board gets it and that your employees can build it?

A writer described practically every detail in that

iconic scene from *The Sound of Music*, trusting a vision of how it should look on film. The writer didn't worry about the ins and outs of *how* it would be achieved. The writer knew those operational aspects of the job would be handled later by the people who specialize in those fields.

The Vivid Vision is like a script: It maps out the future in such a way that everyone who has a role to play understands their role. If the screenwriter had only written a mission statement for that scene, what on Earth would have been the result? Is everyone going to be on the same page knowing exactly what that statement means? Of course not.

A vision board at least resembles a storyboard, but there is a reason that screenplays, and not storyboards, serve as the skeleton of a movie. A storyboard would not provide the unambiguous descriptions necessary to that scene, such as the music, song lyrics, camera directions, and so on.

Again, apart from you, no one in your organization knows with any certainty what it is you intend to make of the company you lead. And they can't build it, if they can't see it. It's your task to provide them with the means of seeing it. And if you don't, we're right back to the old tale of the blind men and the elephant.

TRUST THE PROCESS

Maybe this is your first time hearing of a Vivid Vision. I'm sure you're familiar with mission statements and vision boards, but as I have pointed out, those tools are so vague and ambiguous as to be completely ineffective.

My hope is that you will trust the process that I have laid out in this book, believing it to be a helpful and useful instrument.

If you only dip a toe in the water—thinking too small, planning only a year or two out, considering the operational obstacles—you will not experience the full benefits that this resource can provide. On the flip side, if you go too far out in the vision—imagining a future ten or twenty years out with goals that are so audacious as to be entirely out of the realm of possibility—then you will have wasted an afternoon daydreaming.

The mission statement and the vision board were once radical new ideas that nobody had considered before. They were no doubt scoffed at as being far-out at first. Old-fashioned business leaders would have stuck to their three-word mottos—like "integrity, trust, stability"—or other such outdated ways of explaining their core values.

Eventually, of course, enough companies began adopting the practice of assembling longer explanations—mission statements and, later, vision boards—that it became a ubiquitous component of any organization.

Just as the mission statement inevitably replaced the motto, more and more businesses and individuals are beginning to implement the Vivid Vision. It's the Vivid Vision that gives them tangible results. At some point, it will likely hit critical mass and replace the essentially senseless mission statement and the unintelligible vision board.

But until that time comes, I ask you to trust me. Trust the process that I've successfully coached other leaders through. Trust me that there is a better way of aligning and guiding your business as a cohesive organism moving in lockstep toward identifiable and achievable Big, Hairy, Audacious Goals.

All you need to do is trust the process, and that Big, Hairy, Audacious Goal will be yours to realize, too.

ABOUT THE AUTHOR

CAMERON HEROLD has taken twenty years of experience operating some of the biggest business success stories in North America and turned it into a flourishing career as both a business consultant and a motivational speaker. Cameron is a business coach and mentor to several fast-growth businesses and a CEO coach to large corporations throughout Canada and the United States.

"Book In A Box was an incredible experience. All I had to do was talk about what I know, they did the rest, and the book is exactly what I wanted it to be."

—CAMERON HEROLD

IT'S TIME TO WRITE YOUR BOOK

Cameron spent the first half of his life building and scaling companies, and he was very good at that. He decided to spend the second half of his life helping other people achieve their dreams, and dedicated himself to teaching what he learned to entrepreneurs and CEOs.

What he didn't want to do was spend that time slaving away at a keyboard. He knew he had multiple books in him, but he couldn't find the time to sit down, type them out, and go through the whole publishing process.

So, just like when he was a CEO or COO and had to find innovative solutions to hard problems, he solved his book problem by working smarter, not harder. He used us.

Book In A Box is a company that turns ideas into books.

We surround our authors with a team of publishing professionals that help clarify and structure their book idea, get their words out of their head (in their voice), and then professionally publish their book, in about 10x less time than if they do it themselves.

Cameron used us for the book you have in your hands (and his two other recent books). And he liked us so much, he came onboard as an advisor (we're learning the same business lessons from him and his books that you are as we grow our company).

If you have valuable ideas in your head as well, and believe they might make a good book, we're happy to talk and see if we can help.

Start here: www.bookinabox.com/CameronHerold

Made in the USA
Coppell, TX
29 June 2021

58316728R00095